Austerity

T0052627

Austerity

Suzanne J. Konzelmann

polity

The right of Suzanne J. Konzelmann to be identified as Author of this Work has been asserted in accordance with the UK Copyright, Designs and Patents Act 1988.

First published in 2019 by Polity Press

Polity Press
65 Bridge Street
Cambridge CB2 1UR, UK

Polity Press
101 Station Landing
Suite 300
Medford, MA 02155, USA

ISBN-13: 978-1-5095-3486-9
ISBN-13: 978-1-5095-3487-6 (pb)

A catalogue record for this book is available from the British Library.

Library of Congress Cataloging-in-Publication Data

Names: Konzelmann, Suzanne J., author.
Title: Austerity / Suzanne J. Konzelmann.
Description: Cambridge, UK ; Medford, MA : Polity, 2019. | Includes bibliographical references and index.
Identifiers: LCCN 2019006572 (print) | LCCN 2019009886 (ebook) | ISBN 9781509534883 (Epub) | ISBN 9781509534869 (hardback) | ISBN 9781509534876 (pbk.)
Subjects: LCSH: Economic policy. | Economic history. | Debts, Public.
Classification: LCC HD87 (ebook) | LCC HD87 .K663 2019 (print) | DDC 336.3–dc23
LC record available at https://lccn.loc.gov/2019006572

Typeset in 10.5 on 12 pt Sabon
by Toppan Best-set Premedia Limited
Printed and bound in Great Britain by TJ International Limited

For further information on Polity, visit our website: politybooks.com

Contents

1
Introduction

Introduction

Austerity has become a widely used term in economic poli-cymaking circles, academic research, and the popular media, since concerns were raised about high levels of Greek sovereign debt following the 2008 financial crisis. In 2010, it was named "word of the year" by the Merriam Webster Dictionary, after a surge of more than 250,000 searches for the term on its website. However, there is no well worked-out theory of aus-terity in economic thought; and it remains a confusing and poorly understood concept.

Before World War II, austerity was primarily used to refer to harsh physical conditions and/or rationing. Yet during the turbulent interwar years, the British economist and Treasury advisor, John Maynard Keynes, famously argued that "[t]he boom, not the slump, is the right time for austerity at the Treasury."[1] From this perspective, austerity is the necessary counterpart to a policy of economic stimulus, to be prag-matically applied when the economy appears "stuck" in one phase of the economic cycle or another. More recently – and especially since the 2008 financial crisis – austerity has been used to describe government deficit reduction policies involving spending cuts (and sometimes tax increases). However, it has also been used for political and ideological reasons (stated or not), as a means of reducing the size and economic role of the state, particularly with respect to social welfare provision.

While most contemporary austerity policies have similar overall (stated) objectives – reducing a government's commitment to both its annual deficit (if there is one) and (eventually) the level of public debt – there is significant variation in the specific measures involved; there is also a lack of consensus about which policies qualify as austerity measures. Nonetheless, the merits of generalized austerity continue to be the subject of intense political, economic, and social debate.

Although the aims of austerity policies and attitudes toward public debt have changed relatively little since they were first introduced – as we will see in Chapter 2, as well as in the comparative case studies presented later on – the social, economic and political context within which both austerity and debt now operate has evolved beyond all recognition. The uses to which national debt has been put have also significantly changed, particularly as governments have assumed responsibility for an expanding range of services, including social security, the cost of which fluctuates with shifts in the economic cycle and population demographics.

The dynamics of austerity policy have also evolved, and its effects have become more complex and wide-ranging as a result of political and socioeconomic developments and the shifting role of the state. At the same time, attitudes toward both personal and business debt have also moved on, as – especially since the 1970s collapse of the Bretton Woods international monetary system – the vastly expanded supply of available credit has permitted significant increases in both public and private debt as well as the leverage of globalized financial institutions.

However, despite radical changes in the context within which it operates, as we will see in Chapter 3, the *economics* of austerity (or stimulus) is fairly uncomplicated; and its likely impact on government accounts – in general terms, at least – is relatively easy to anticipate. Austerity's effect on the economy, however, while being *technically* straightforward to predict, will vary considerably according to the phase of the economic cycle in which it is implemented. The use of austerity to cool an overheating economy, for example, is likely to have more beneficial effects than if implemented when an economy is in recession – which is generally defined as a fall in Gross Domestic Product (GDP) for two consecutive quarters

– with political and social factors playing an important role in such decisions.

The *political and social* dimensions of austerity, however, are more complex in terms of their influence and outcomes than the economic dimensions. The combined effect of economic, political, and social factors both on austerity and on the outcomes resulting from it must therefore be set into the context of how national accounting actually works, what impact differences in economic performance are likely to have, and how changes in the government's economic activity might influence the dynamics of the system. Only then can the less predictable, political, and social aspects of austerity be factored into the analysis.

Like the aims and primary components of austerity itself, as we will see in Chapter 4, many of the arguments used to garner political and/or public support for it have changed remarkably little since the times of Adam Smith, Jean-Baptiste Say, and the classical political economists. While these arguments may well have made economic sense when first advanced, most have since been overtaken by the evolution of political economy – notably the appearance of so-called "automatic stabilizers" – which can significantly affect the outcome of a program of austerity. As a result, many of these arguments are now open to debate.

Thus, while, on the face of it, when public debt levels are high, austerity might seem intuitively appealing and entirely sensible, even a cursory analysis reveals that cutting net public expenditure is likely to have a number of other, rather less desirable, results; and depending upon the political and socioeconomic context, it may well *not* have the desired effect on a government's deficit and debt –at the time of writing, indeed, it has not done so.

Overview of the Book

This book explores the economic, political, and sociocultural dimensions of austerity, as both an idea and a policy, through the basic mechanics of national accounting as well as comparative political and socioeconomic history from the seventeenth century onward, when the concept of "national debt" in the modern sense first emerged. Examining a range of comparative case studies, from the interwar years to the present, austerity's outcomes will be evaluated against its stated objectives, as will alternative policies under similar economic conditions.

The political economic, ideological, and sociocultural reasons behind both support for and opposition to austerity as a policy will be assessed, with a clear demarcation between critiques based on the implications of austerity for macroeconomic performance, output and growth, on the one hand, and those based on its sociopolitical implications in terms of distributional and social outcomes (such as poverty, inequality, and health), on the other. The book's overall aim is to demystify the concept of austerity, as both an economic idea and an approach to policy.

Chapter 2 locates austerity within its broader historical and theoretical context, tracing shifting reactions to the evolution of national debt – and the economic role of the state – since its first appearance during the late seventeenth century through to the present. We then explore the *economics* of austerity through the lens of national accounting in Chapter 3. Chapter 4 assesses the arguments that have recently been marshaled in support of austerity as a deliberate economic policy – as well as the counterarguments that have been made.

With these historical, analytical, and theoretical ideas in mind, in Chapters 5 through 8, we turn to a comparative analysis of the experiences of countries that, since World War I, either embraced austerity to confront the economic and political challenges they faced, or had it forced upon them as a condition for financial assistance. We will also examine cases where governments have chosen an alternative path to austerity. Our aim is to assess the outcomes realized in the light of the objectives, stated or otherwise. From this, it becomes clear that the question is not whether austerity is "good" or "bad" – or whether it benefits or damages economic growth – but rather, in what circumstances austerity might be deemed appropriate; and when it is more likely to be seen as counterproductive.

Chapter 9 considers the political economic, ideological, and sociocultural dimensions of austerity as a way of making sense of its tenaciousness, despite the policy's repeated failure to deliver on its promises. Chapter 10 concludes.

2

Shifting Responses to the Evolution of National Debt and the Economic Role of the State

Introduction

Austerity is inextricably connected to the question of debt; so to understand austerity – attempts to reduce or eliminate government debt – it is essential to consider not only its co-evolution with the concept of a "national debt," but also the nature and development of the political and socioeconomy within which this is taking place.

This chapter traces the evolution of ideas about economic austerity – many of which resonate with contemporary ones – in the context of shifting political, economic, and social events accompanying the development of market, industrial, and financial capitalism. It examines the changing nature of the state – from that ruled by a monarch to a more democratic form of government – and markets, in which the role of the state and its relationship with markets and society come to the fore. In this context, the idea of austerity can be linked to the question of the appropriate means of funding both the state – via taxation and/or borrowing – and the national debt.

Origins of National Debt – and Austerity

The roots of austerity can be traced to the late seventeenth century and the birth of "national debt" in its modern form.

Although markets for sovereign debt had emerged in Venice, Florence, and other Italian city republics during the fifteenth century – and spread throughout Europe, to Spain, France, and Holland – it was Britain's "Glorious Revolution" (1688–9) and the political dominance of its rich upper-class elite that ushered in a more orderly system of government borrowing.

By the 1690s, England had emerged from a major civil war, but was facing both a poor credit rating and a need to raise significant funds, in part to build a more powerful navy. King Charles I (1600–49) had imposed heavy taxes in order to fund the construction of warships – one of many factors leading to the civil war (and, hence, the King's execution). The scale of the funds required for the latest naval project thus clearly suggested that financing it through taxation might well be fraught with problems. As a result, the new King, William III (1650–1702; also known as William of Orange), was keen to find an alternative means of finance. The solution was a loan of £1.2 million to the English government, funded by private subscription on agreed terms, from the newly established Bank of England, which was set up in 1694 as a private company, approved and authorized by Royal Charter. Many of the initial investors – then, as now – were from overseas, particularly the Netherlands, where relations with England had warmed considerably since the Glorious Revolution had put William and Mary on the English throne.

Under William of Orange, the stability of the British political system created such confidence in the government's debt that it was able to borrow large sums at lower rates than those paid by private borrowers and other governments, offering considerable advantages; it also fostered fiscal prudence to maintain the confidence of the money markets. As other major economies took note of the advantages of this approach to government finance, it was soon adopted elsewhere.

Imperial expansion, the first industrial revolution – and the "classical" debate about austerity

With the birth of modern national debt, large amounts of funds were available to drive both imperial expansion and industrial development across much of the Western world.

The resulting industrial revolution transformed economies and spurred domestic and international growth; and from the early eighteenth century, following Britain's lead, the major European countries also embarked on imperial expansion. Successful wars for this purpose, although initially incurring public debt, usually became self-funding, since the gains in natural resources, markets, and tax revenues typically surpassed the costs of securing them. However, the new colonies then needed to be defended, maintained, and administered; these costs were less easy to recoup, especially if the colonies revolted against taxation, as the Americans had done during the War of Independence (1775–83). The unpopularity of taxation, its short-term nature and tendency to provoke unrest thus encouraged alternative methods of public financing; and with these developments came new ideas and theories about government spending and public debt – as well as austerity.

In addition to economic and social change, the eighteenth and nineteenth centuries brought significant advances in science and engineering, including the ideas of Isaac Newton, Charles Darwin, and Marie and Pierre Curie – to name but a few. The flood of significant discoveries in the pure and applied sciences suggested to some that science might well have something to offer economic theory, especially in the context of the radical changes wrought by the industrial revolution, the seismic shifts in society, and the financial development that accompanied it. Ever since, economics has aspired to be a "real science," like physics.

The early stages of the industrial revolution set off a transformation of formerly agrarian economies into more urban, mobile, cash-based – and often volatile – ones. At this point, national debt was still in its infancy, mostly financing short- to medium-term military activities. As a result, rather than being intimately connected with the *economic* cycle, it was mainly linked to a *war and peace* cycle. Since wars were generally of a short – or, at least, finite – duration, national debt, too, was seen as a temporary, rather than an ongoing, commitment.

For the political economists of the time, fiscal policy was all about balancing the budget; anything else was considered economically destabilizing. Frugality was a cardinal virtue, which was reflected in the widely accepted principle that government budgets should be in balance, if not in surplus, and that deficits could only be tolerated in situations such as war. Substantial and continuing deficits – particularly during peacetime – were the mark of fiscal folly.

The classical debate about austerity mainly revolved around whether to finance public spending through taxation or borrowing. The fundamental difference was the timing of the payments: taxation put the burden on taxpayers during the period of expenditure, while debt postponed it until the interest and amortization payments became due. Debt financing thus shifted the burden of payment, possibly onto future generations; the question was therefore about who should shoulder the burden of the debt – and when.

The Dutch economist Isaac de Pinto (1717–87) was an early contributor to this debate. A merchant banker of Jewish descent – and one of the main investors in the Dutch East India Company – he felt that sovereign debt might have wider advantages. In his *Traité de la Circulation et du Crédit*, de Pinto argued that national debt and stock market speculation in securities played a potentially positive role by fostering credit, increasing the circulation of money, and promoting economic well-being.

This contrasted sharply with the view of the eighteenth-century British economists David Hume (1711–76) and Adam Smith (1723–90), who were both concerned about England's sovereign debt, which was a result of mercantile expansion – and what they considered the "degeneracy" associated with public borrowing. They argued that debt financing of mercantilist activities by government was not only evidence of profligacy; it also imposed fiscal burdens on future generations of taxpayers, while interest payments on public debt transferred money away from "productive labor" to "maintaining unproductive labor."[1]

Writing at the beginning of the industrial revolution, as well as the union of England and Scotland, Smith, a middle-class professor of moral philosophy and a tax official, noted the economic and social benefits, as well as the radical changes brought about by the industrial revolution. At this point, state debt was still largely accumulated to finance military activities; and it was long before the appearance of what would later come to be known as "automatic stabilizers" – spending on social welfare (which automatically increases during recessions and decreases during booms) and income tax receipts (which do the opposite). This meant that the national debt in those days could be far more realistically compared to domestic or commercial budgets than it can today. Public debt could, under peacetime conditions, be paid down with little or no political or economic downside. It is therefore not surprising that early theorists saw this as a fairly obvious comparison. In *The Wealth of Nations*, for example, Smith drew the analogy between a private family and a government budget: "What is prudence in the conduct of every private family, can scarce be folly in that of a great kingdom."[2]

The French economist and businessman Jean-Baptiste Say (1767–1832) – famous for "Say's Law," the idea that "supply creates its own demand" – also compared a private to a public budget. Like Smith, Say believed that just as a family that wishes to prosper must avoid spending more than it earns, a government that wishes its nation to prosper must avoid spending in excess of its tax revenues, so as to leave resources for the private sector to invest. From this perspective, there is a danger in borrowing and accumulating debt because an indebted nation, with high and mounting interest payments, like a private household or business, can become bankrupt. Thus, the government budget should be balanced except in extraordinary circumstances.

"Crowding-out" – where state borrowing competes with the private sector for limited credit, pushing up its price in the process – was another idea in support of a minimal level of public debt. When financial systems were still at an early stage of development, with credit far more limited than it is at present, "crowding-out" would have made economic sense. However, during the course of the twentieth century, this would cease to be the case, with abandonment of the gold standard and the removal of restrictions on international capital flows. But as we will see in later chapters, like the comparison between state and domestic budgets, the "crowding-out" argument has not only lingered on into the twenty-first century, it is inherent to the current debate, despite the fact that here, too, economic and financial circumstances have radically moved-on – in this case as a consequence of an exponential increase in the supply of global credit.

The American statesman and one of the founding fathers of the United States, Alexander Hamilton (1757–1804), was another contributor to the debate about austerity and public debt. Following the American Revolution (1775–83), during which the newly independent American colonies had accumulated enormous debts, Hamilton, the first Treasury Secretary, was requested by Congress in 1789 to prepare a report analyzing the state of the new country's finances. His plan for retiring the national debt aimed to inspire investor confidence in the new nation's solvency. This was outlined in Hamilton's *First Report on Public Credit*, which proposed a "debt assessment plan" by which all debts would be repaid at face value. The federal government would assume responsibility for the debts of the states, which would be financed by issuing interest-bearing bonds that could be used as collateral for securing further loans. In contrast to Smith and Hume – and leaning more towards de Pinto – Hamilton reasoned that by *funding* the debt (rather than paying off the principal as quickly as possible), and allowing creditors to secure further loans against their investments in government bonds, the plan would encourage investment in government securities, which, in turn, would transform the debt into a source of capital and stimulate the economy.

Writing up to a century after Smith and Hume, the English economist David Ricardo (1772–1823) was a Member of Parliament, but, perhaps most influentially, also a financier who had made his fortune speculating on government debt – especially debt raised to fund the Waterloo campaign. During the Napoleonic Wars (1803–15), Britain accumulated enormous debt; however, despite the source of his newly made fortune, Ricardo referred to debt as "one of the most terrible scourges which was ever invented to afflict a nation."[3] By this time, industrialization was far more advanced than when Hume and Smith were writing, and government borrowing was no longer portrayed as necessarily threatening to economic progress; indeed, it was generally regarded more favorably.

Ricardo's interest focused on ways of financing public expenditure. In his *Essay on the Funding System*, he examined the relative "equivalence" of financing a war by means of taxation or by the issuing of government bonds. Although he concluded that there was no real difference, he doubted the practical significance of his conclusion because if people indeed had "rational expectations," they would be indifferent about how a war was paid for. However, since they were likely to oppose additional taxes – favoring borrowing instead – their decisions would be distorted by this "fiscal illusion." Ricardo therefore concluded that "during peace, our unceasing efforts should be directed towards paying off that part of the debt which has been contracted during war."[4] Ricardo's preference for debt over tax seems to have been borne out by the initial responses to early forms of income tax, which, if anything, raised even more ire than the idea of a national debt.

Income tax – and the first appearance of an "automatic stabilizer"

The twentieth century has been seen as the era of the "tax state," as a result of the unprecedented pace of expansion of government budgets across the developed world. However, during the nineteenth century, as industrialization progressed – and especially during the second industrial revolution (1870–1914) – states began to assume responsibility for an increasing number of commitments in addition to financing wars, including infrastructure development and improvements in the provision of public education, health, and old-age pensions. This introduced longer term spending into the government's budget.

To finance these "structural" components of the state's budget, politicians looked for additional sources of public revenue; so taxes were imposed not only on property, but also on windows, doors, buildings, luxuries, matches, and consumption – all of which provided public revenue streams that were relatively stable across the economic cycle. Proposals to adopt a tax on income were also put forward. But they tended to be met with strong skepticism and opposition – especially in countries such as the USA, France, and Germany, which had established extensive suffrage rules early on. By contrast, countries that had very limited suffrage – such as the UK, Austria, and Italy – introduced income taxes much earlier.

Britain was the first country to adopt a permanent income tax in 1842. A precursor had been introduced in 1798 to pay for weapons and equipment in preparation for the Napoleonic Wars of 1803–15. The tax was levied from 1799 to 1802, but was abolished during the Treaty of Amiens, which temporarily ended hostilities between the French Republic and Britain. However, it was reintroduced in 1803 when war broke out again.

Unsurprisingly, this new tax was at least as unpopular as national debt; and when it was repealed in 1816, a year after the Battle of Waterloo, opponents of the tax, who thought that it should only be used to help finance wars, pressured Parliament to order the destruction of all documents connected with it. These were publicly burned by the Chancellor of the Exchequer, although copies were retained in the basement of the tax court. Attempts to abolish income taxes altogether would prove futile; and it was not long before they returned – eventually on a permanent basis.

In the United States, during the War of 1812, the first income tax – based on the British Tax Act of 1798 – was proposed and developed in 1814. But it was never imposed because the 1815 Treaty of Ghent ended both hostilities and the need for additional revenue. It was not until President Lincoln signed the Tax Act of 1862, to help finance the Civil War, that an American income tax was actually levied. But even then, only a small fraction of the population filed a tax return; and at the war's end, income tax was declared unconstitutional, being replaced by significant tariffs, which served as an important source of government revenue until the outbreak of World War I in 1914. The income tax imposed in 1913 was also limited in its reach, with exemptions relieving virtually all of the middle classes from paying it. By one estimate, only 2 percent of American households were subject to the tax, with even the wealthy paying marginal rates of between 1 and 7 percent.

Similarly, in France, repeated attempts to adopt an income tax during the nineteenth century were met with such strong opposition that it, too, was effectively delayed until the start of World War I. Because the French Revolution had been fueled in part by anger against tax collectors, the system was designed to limit direct contact between tax collectors and payers. Thus, the main revenues came from taxes on things that were easily assessed, such as real estate, doors, windows, and consumption.

The linking of tax revenues to personal income – rather than fixed assets or consumption – represented the first of what would later become known as "automatic stabilizers." Government income from taxes would now rise more sharply during a boom, when incomes were rising – and drop further and faster during a slump, when unemployment caused incomes to fall. This linking of a country's national income to the state of its economy came with a significant downside, since financial crises were also part and parcel of economic and industrial development – which was increasingly dependent upon an expanded financial services sector. However, as there was still no significant commitment to social welfare spending, recessions were not yet subject to a full set of automatic stabilizers in the modern sense of the term. During a slump, tax receipts might well go down, but it would be nearly a century before rising welfare costs would factor into the equation.

This is not to say that there was no pressure for the government to pay attention to social welfare, since it was becoming increasingly difficult to continue to ignore the large numbers of urban poor. A combination of pressure for a fairer voting system – and where that failed, the threat of socialist revolution – would soon transform the political and economic landscape. Thus, socioeconomic developments would become increasingly influential in both politics and economic thought – and eventually, by extension, austerity.

Social consequences of industrialization

Once industrialization hit its stride, spreading beyond Britain to new and larger economies such as the United States, it wasn't just international competition that intensified: both cities and the numbers of the urban poor expanded exponentially. For a time, government spending was still largely confined to military activities, which, in theory, were relatively short-term commitments – with the implication that, so too, was the debt incurred. But as the industrial revolution progressed, the growing numbers of dispossessed people (with very little to lose), would become an increasingly potent force, both physically (because of their sheer numbers) and politically (with extension of the franchise) – and one that could not easily be ignored.

A contemporary of Ricardo, Thomas Malthus (1766–1834) was a cleric as well as a scholar. Having experienced the first industrial revolution – and witnessed its effects on the growing numbers of poor – his *Essay on the Principle of Population* was an early work connecting economic development with population growth. Both Malthus's ideas and the social effects of the industrial revolution were brought vividly to life in the works of the novelist Charles Dickens (1812–70), who, in *A Christmas Carol*, put Malthus's views on population into the mouth of Ebenezer Scrooge.

With respect to public debt, Malthus saw things differently from Ricardo. In his *Principles of Political Economy*, Malthus argued that those living on the interest from the national debt – Smith's and Hume's "idle rich" – "contribute powerfully to distribution and demand … they ensure effective consumption, which is necessary to give the proper stimulus to production."[5] Because he believed that employment and incomes for the many depend upon the powers of production, Malthus felt "it would be the height of folly to determine, under all circumstances, that the sudden diminution of the national debt and the removal of taxation must necessarily tend to increase the national wealth, and provide employment for the working classes."[6] Attributing the stagnation that followed the Napoleonic Wars to under-consumption following the cessation of wartime demand, Malthus recommended moderating the pace at which wartime debts were retired, going so far as to suggest that, if all else failed, the government should impose taxes and spend the proceeds – restoring the balance between demand and supply. This was an important insight that John Maynard Keynes would later build upon.

John Stuart Mill (1806–73), whose father was a close friend of Ricardo, was a British philosopher, political economist, and civil servant. One of the most influential thinkers in the history of liberalism, he took a position between that of Ricardo and Malthus. Mill's conception of liberty justified the freedom of the individual as opposed to unlimited state and social control. While a supporter of free markets, he also thought that government intervention was justified in the interest of society as whole. In *Of National Debt*, Mill defended public debt to counter under-consumption, when "some amount of national debt is desirable, and almost indispensable, as an investment for the savings of the poorer or more inexperienced part of the community." However, he also believed that public borrowing was potentially harmful as it absorbed capital that could otherwise be used for production and employment. Thus, in answering the question of whether it is "expedient to take steps for redeeming that debt," Mill contended that "in principle, it is impossible not to maintain the affirmative."

After Mill, national debt was less controversial for a while, given that, in the advanced economies, it remained relatively low and stable until the outbreak of World War I in 1914. Although the usual debates about the effects of government spending, the rate at which debt should be retired, and how to finance it all continued, there was general agreement that, except in extraordinary circumstances, every effort should be made to maintain a balance (if not a surplus) in the government budget.

Karl Marx (1818–83), however, had a very different perspective from those of the distinctly middle-class theorists of his time, having witnessed the socialist ideas and movements of the mid-nineteenth century – when "revolution" was, quite literally, all the rage in many parts of Europe and the Americas. During this period, Marx moved from country to country, as necessity and political circumstance dictated – giving him a very international perspective. Surrounded by other socialists, his viewpoint – including his ideas about national debt – was significantly shaped by his experiences:

> The public debt becomes one of the most powerful levers of primitive accumulation. As with the stroke of an enchanter's wand, it endows unproductive money with the power of creation and thus turns it into capital, without forcing it to expose itself to the troubles and risks inseparable for its employment in industry, or even in usury. The state's creditors actually give nothing away, for the sum lent is transformed into public bonds, easily negotiable which go on functioning in their hands just as so much hard cash would.[7]

Marx went on to show the importance of the founding of the Bank of England and the trading in public debt for the establishment and growth of banks and other financial institutions "in the capitalization of wealth and the expropriation of the masses" and hence the development of British capitalism.[8] Largely in response to the direction in which Marxist analysis was taking classical economics, the "marginal revolution" of the late nineteenth century produced the "neoclassical" school, which discarded the social and political elements of classical economics and divorced economic theorizing from its historical context. Instead, economics was increasingly presented as a "science" that addressed universal principles, attempting to emulate advances in physics, biology, and chemistry. Neoclassical economists emphasized the primacy of markets in determining relative prices and income distribution; and they were skeptical about taxation and government spending, seeing them as misdirecting market forces.

Permanent state commitments: a game-changer for national debt and austerity

The industrial revolution had brought widespread social and economic change that would further influence the direction of theory and policy with respect to the economics of austerity. In addition to economic growth, industrialization gave rise to major social problems, especially mass urban poverty. However, the traditional emphasis on *individual* freedom and responsibility meant that societal needs were not given much policy priority.

This slowly began to change as the political franchise – generally limited to property-owning, tax-paying white males – widened. Although suffrage was not extended to women until after World Wars I and II, by the close of the nineteenth century, across the industrializing world, extension of male suffrage, regardless of income, property, religion, race, or any other qualification, meant that political parties had to solicit working-class support at the polls.

As a result, the early twentieth century brought not only increased public spending on such things as roads, but also early experiments with social welfare. These were driven to a large extent by nervousness about socialist revolution – especially following events associated with the Russian revolutions of 1905 and 1917 – as well as by the increasing political influence of the newly enfranchised poor. This sharply increased the political dimension of austerity, since its effects usually fall disproportionately on those most reliant on government services.

However, while this politicization of austerity would be significant, perhaps even more so was the introduction of a full set of automatic stabilizers. With the adoption of social welfare programs came increased costs during recessions, in addition to the problem of lower tax receipts. This appreciably changed the social, economic, and political dynamics of recessions and booms – and, as a result, the dynamics of austerity.

While nineteenth-century legislation had attempted (albeit without much success) to deal with urban poverty, the speed of the transition from an agrarian to an urban-based industrial economy led to a sharp deterioration in living and working conditions – especially during the second half of the century. As what remained of the old social order disappeared, increasing numbers of people faced difficulties subsisting in what was becoming an exclusively cash-driven economy, with the uncertainties of fluctuating prices, insecure employment, and poor prospects, especially for those surviving long enough to be too old to work. The appalling conditions suffered by the working classes during the industrial revolution generated widespread social and industrial unrest – so much so that political parties evolved to accommodate, channel, and ultimately represent the interests of the new urban proletariat.

During the 1880s, the Chancellor of the German Empire, Otto von Bismarck (1815–98), responded to the challenges of rapid industrialization – and the rising strength of the industrial proletariat – by initiating a process of social reform. Opposed to socialism, Bismarck's program centered on insurance programs – covering sickness, accidents, and disability – and a retirement pension. These were designed to provide workers with greater security, thereby increasing productivity and stimulating economic growth – and focusing their political attention on things other than revolution.

In Britain, the fledgling Labour Party emerged to join the established two-party political system. This sudden visibility of the working classes ratcheted up fears of uncontrollable social change, producing a split in the British Liberal party.

While some felt that state intervention in free markets was still the biggest threat to civil liberty, a significant group, including David Lloyd George (1863–1945) and Winston Churchill (1874–1965), saw the concentration of capital and socialist revolution as the more important threats – a view that the Russian Revolution in 1905 did little to dispel. But rather than experiment with radical change, the British government took its inspiration from von Bismarck, and, between 1906 and 1913, a succession of social legislation was enacted, such that by 1914, aside from the National Health Service (NHS), the British social welfare state was largely in place.

The progress of the social reform movement was, however, halted by the ruinously expensive World War I (1914–18), which renewed the debate about the vastly expanded public debt of the countries involved, and put "austerity" center stage. However, the increased spending on social welfare significantly politicized the issue, since any reduction in funding would be likely to result in a negative reaction on the part of voters – many of whom by then had military experience. It would thus be necessary to "sell" the idea of austerity rather more carefully.

The "Keynesian" Challenge: Austerity in "The Boom, Not the Slump"

Britain emerged from World War I victorious, but economically weak, and, after a brief but hectic boom, the economy fell into depression. The government responded by reverting to prewar laissez-faire economic policy. Public expenditure was reduced in an effort to balance the budget and return Britain to the gold standard. A concerted effort was also made to repay large wartime loans, and monetary policy was targeted at defending sterling. Continued high unemployment and balance of payments deficits were blamed on the war, which had disrupted export markets and radically increased production costs. The Treasury therefore reasoned that a return to economic "normality" required wage cuts to restore prices to their prewar levels.

However, efforts to cut wages were fiercely resisted by the trade unions; and industrial militancy intensified, rekindling the fear of socialism that had been triggered by the latest (1917) Russian revolution. However, despite the ensuing economic, social, and political unrest, high unemployment, and persistent balance-of-payments deficits, the Treasury doggedly pursued its austerity policy, but with very little success as far as reducing the national debt was concerned.

This attempt to return to "normal" prewar policies was ultimately derailed by the fact that the old "normal" had been replaced by an entirely new reality. Although the effect of an abrupt drop in demand following the end of a major war had been seen before, the effect of the now complete set of automatic stabilizers hadn't. In the face of a recession, where confidence was low and unemployment high, there were new dynamics to grapple with. Any commitment to social welfare – felt to be essential in limiting tendencies towards extremism – would now increase government costs during a recession. This was not the end of the misery though, as the state's increasing reliance on income tax (rather than property or consumption taxes) meant that, at the same time as unemployment-related social welfare costs were going up, tax receipts were going down – a recipe for increasing public deficits and debt, rather than reducing them. This, in turn, would have serious implications for austerity, which would now come with unwelcome – and apparently inexplicable – side effects.

These new dynamics required entirely new theories to both explain them and provide the foundation for developing policies to deal with them – marking a step change from the economy that the classical political economists had been theorizing. The game had moved on.

John Maynard Keynes (1883–1946) – who also had considerable experience as a financial investor, civil servant, political actor, and policy advisor – was among the first to recognize the changed environment. In a direct challenge to the "Treasury view" – that state borrowing and spending put the government into competition with the private sector, but create no permanent additional employment – he argued that the solution to Britain's economic problems lay not in austerity but in stimulus, aimed at increasing home demand to compensate for shrinking export markets. From this perspective, the cure for unemployment involves *both* monetary reform *and* major public works expenditure, financed by borrowing. In Keynes's analysis, the *timing* of stimulus and austerity is key, with austerity (both monetary and fiscal) being the necessary counterpart to stimulus, to be applied during the boom – and *not* during the recession – to help avoid the risk of inflation or financial collapse and build up the resources for dealing with the next economic slump.

Keynes however, was not the only voice advocating government intervention to stabilize the economy – nor was he the first.

American "pre-Keynesians"

The United States had emerged from World War I in much better shape than Britain, with a massively stronger economy and having assumed a position of financial hegemony. Between 1922 and 1929, the US economy grew rapidly and employment remained high. However, this was not confined to the level of expenditure and the way the economy was organized; it was also related to the way the economy was theorized. In economics, there had developed a "vigorous, diverse and distinctly American literature dealing with monetary economics and the business cycle."[9] It was essentially institutional; and, unlike in Britain, there was little opposition to countercyclical fiscal and monetary policy – increased government spending and tax cuts during recessions, and austerity during booms. There was, however, considerable debate about its effectiveness and how public spending should be financed. The main centers for these ideas were Harvard (where Lauchlin Currie, Paul Ellsworth, and Harry Dexter White were important) and Chicago (where contributors included Aaron Director, Paul Douglas, Frank Knight, Henry Simons, and Jacob Viner).

In many ways the American institutionalists anticipated Keynes's ideas, particularly with regard to stabilizing the economic cycle. The Great Depression added urgency to this debate, with the Chicago economist, Paul Douglas, making the case for public works, to be financed by monetary expansion on the grounds that "it is possible for government to

increase the demand for labor without a corresponding contraction of private demand and ... this is particularly the case
when fresh monetary purchasing power is created to finance
the construction work."[10] The Americans thus preferred money
creation to finance government deficit spending, because it
injected new liquidity and did not incur an interest charge or
increase the rate of interest. Also, as long as inflation remained
manageable, it might also have a greater expansionary effect
than debt financing, since bond sales to the public leave them
with less money to spend.

By 1933, when the Franklin Roosevelt administration came
to office, the US was suffering "from the most extreme pros-
tration which any capitalist country had ever experienced in
peace time."[11] Informed by the economists at the Universities
of Harvard and Chicago, the "New Deal" reforms of 1933
through 1937 were enacted. Under this deliberately expansionary policy, the American economy recovered. But fear of
inflation checked New Deal expansionism, slowing the recovery,
and in 1937, pressure to reduce the fiscal deficit brought a
brief return to austerity. The sharp recession that resulted
almost returned the economy to depression, but with the
stimulus provided by rearmament and World War II (1939–45),
the economy fully recovered.

Postwar commitment to "Keynesian" ideas about deficit spending – and public debt

The massive stimulus to aggregate demand, provided by World
War II, seemed to justify the ideas of both the American
institutionalists and Keynes about the role of the state in
managing the economy; it also re-established confidence in
the West that capitalism could be restored. Whereas the classical and neoclassical economists had focused on the effects
of government borrowing and spending on the *budget* – so-
called "sound finance" – "Keynesians" instead focused on
their effects on the *economy* – the new fiscal theory of "functional finance." According to the economist Abba Lerner, "[t]
he central idea is that government fiscal policy ... shall all be
undertaken with an eye only to the *results* of these actions
on the economy and not to any established traditional doctrine
about what is sound or unsound."[12]

During the decades following World War II, the industrialized world enjoyed steady economic expansion; and public debts accumulated during the war were progressively paid off. Governments assumed a central role in managing the macroeconomy, with a widespread commitment to full employment and the welfare state. Financial institutions were either brought into state ownership or more tightly regulated to ensure that they channeled capital to the productive side of the economy, rather than speculation. Domestically, there were quantitative and qualitative controls on credit to maintain price and employment stability; and the Bretton Woods system (1944–71) was established to stabilize the international economic environment, foster world trade, and create the conditions for national governments to more effectively manage their welfare states. International capital flows were strictly controlled; foreign exchange rates were stabilized by pegging currencies to the dollar, which itself was backed by gold; and long-term rates of interest were low, fostering private investment.

All of this helped to lay the foundations for high wage, mass production industrial economies, in which prices were stabilized and greater accord was maintained between capital and labor. The result, especially from 1952 to 1960, was full-employment, low-inflationary growth, rapidly rising living standards, and declining inequality – with virtually no financial crises.

Globalization, Deregulation, and Datasets: Austerity's Evolution During the Late Twentieth and Early Twenty-first Centuries

The twentieth century also brought globalization; and following the collapse of the Bretton Woods monetary system in 1972, there was a turn to pre-Keynesian "neoliberal" ideas and policies, prioritizing markets over state management of the economy, to varying degrees. The idea of "austerity as policy – cutting the state's budget to stabilize public finances, restore competitiveness through wage cuts and create better investment expectations by lowering future tax burdens"[13]

– was revived; and the international financial services sector was steadily deregulated.

The decoupling of the US dollar (and, hence, the basket of other Bretton Woods currencies) from gold – and the financial deregulation of New York and London, respectively, with "May Day" 1976 and "Big Bang" 1985 – resulted in an exponential expansion in the supply of global credit, making the idea of "crowding-out" largely academic. In most OECD countries, private credit substituted for wage growth. Financial corporations led the way, accounting for nearly half of total debt from the early 2000s onward. With monetary policy in the ascendancy, fiscal policy now virtually disappeared as a stabilization device.

Some also felt that the "Great Moderation," from the mid-1980s through 2007 – a period of prolonged expansion and reduced macroeconomic volatility – was proof that monetary policy had indeed conquered the economic cycle. Apparently successful responses to recurring financial crises during the 1980s, 1990s, and 2000s reinforced the view that monetary policy was "well equipped to deal with the financial consequences of asset price busts,"[14] and asset bubbles came to be viewed as legitimate engines for economic growth. Despite the havoc caused when they burst, the dominant view was that bubbles are difficult to identify, so policymakers need not concern themselves with detecting or preventing them. Rather, according to the American economist, Alan Greenspan – who had served as Chairman of the US Federal Reserve from 1987 to 2006 – "it is the job of economic policy-makers to mitigate the fall-out when [the bubble bursts] ... and, hopefully, ease the transition to the next expansion."[15] In this context, calls for austerity accompanied the collapse of successively more serious asset bubbles, on *moral* as well as economic grounds.

Thus, austerity economics shifted, from being a policy for the top of the economic cycle, to prevent inflation and financial crisis, to being one for the bottom, when the excesses of debt-fueled over-consumption reached critical proportions. From this perspective, the 2008 financial crisis is not a spectacular "one-off" incident, but merely the most recent in a series of progressively more serious financial crises requiring public intervention.

The 2008 "global" financial crisis

Despite the neoliberal view that state intervention is economically damaging, during the Great Moderation there was, in fact, *increased* intervention. But its aim was no longer full employment and economic prosperity. Instead, policy was intended to restrain price – if not asset price – inflation and ameliorate financial crises. A significant result was socialization of the risks and costs of financial speculation; another was the moral hazard that came with confidence that the banking system – and financial institutions considered "too big to fail" – would be rescued in the event of crisis. Thus, economic policy, which, prior to the 1980s, had generally served the broader political economy, now increasingly favored the narrow interests of the wealthy and financial elites. Not only the concept of boom and bust, but also countercyclical policy – and therefore the question of austerity versus stimulus – were thus rendered academic. Well, almost.

There is usually much less concern over private debt levels when an economy is performing well; and to many, this was the situation in much of the global economy by the beginning of the twenty-first century – until the "global" financial crisis in 2008. The recession that followed it caused automatic stabilizers to kick in; and governments around the world engaged in emergency fiscal and monetary stimulus. The seemingly inexhaustible supply of credit abruptly dried up; and public debt rose sharply as a consequence of both emergency stimulus measures and the wholesale rescue of systemically important financial institutions. But it did not take long for worsening debt-to-GDP ratios to (allegedly) undermine investor confidence – or for austerity to be demanded as evidence that governments were serious about managing their deficits and repaying their debts.

Public debt, economic stagnation – and
"expansionary austerity"?

The second half of the twentieth century had also produced new ideas about public debt – and, hence, austerity – including those involving computer-based analysis, a tool not available to earlier generations of economists. The evolution of information technology – especially since the mid-1980s – brought the ability to look for patterns and trends in large datasets. However, as with previous debates about austerity, these techniques have failed to provide conclusive evidence about the causal relationship between public debt and macroeconomic outcomes.

Influential contributors included the Harvard economists Carmen Reinhard and Kenneth Rogoff, who had built their academic careers within a largely neoliberal world economy. They had experienced the 1991 collapse of the Soviet Union – and capitalism's apparent victory over socialism and communism – as well as, from an economic perspective, the Great Moderation and 2008 financial crisis. In its aftermath – and especially during the Greek sovereign debt crisis in 2010 – their historical research on financial crises was seized upon by politicians wanting to change course, away from stimulus and toward austerity. This research claimed to show a significant positive correlation between high levels of public debt and economic stagnation – with a public debt "threshold" of 90 percent of GDP at which economic growth contracts.[16]

In his 2010 Mais Lecture, for example, the then UK Chancellor of the Exchequer, George Osborne, contended that, "[a]s Rogoff and Reinhart demonstrate convincingly, all financial crises ultimately have their origins in one thing" – high levels of public debt.[17] In America, Chairman of the House Budget Committee, Congressman Paul Ryan, maintained that "[a] well known study completed by economists Ken Rogoff and Carmen Reinhart confirms a common-sense conclusion. The study found conclusive empirical evidence that gross debt ... exceeding 90 percent of the economy has a significant negative effect on economic growth."[18] And in his address to the ILO on 9 April 2013, Olli Rehn, EU Commissioner for Economic Affairs, used the paper to argue that "in Europe, public debt is expected to stabilize only by 2014 and ... to do so at above the level of 90 percent of GDP. Serious empirical research has shown that at such high levels, public debt acts as a permanent drag on growth."[19]

Once published however, Reinhart and Rogoff's 2010 paper soon faced serious criticism; and its findings were ultimately discredited. Of the various failings cited, perhaps the most significant was the questionable quality of the empirical evidence in which researchers, politicians, and international bureaucrats had placed so much faith. Scholars checking their results soon questioned the dataset, since no one was able to replicate the findings; and when Reinhart and Rogoff eventually allowed access to researchers at the University of Massachusetts Amherst, they discovered omitted data, methodological failings, and Excel coding errors. When these were corrected, the stagnation threshold disappeared. But despite the refutation of their conclusions – and the implications this has had for the austerity programs they were used to justify – Reinhart and Rogoff shrugged it off as "academic kerfuffle,"[20] and policymakers in favor of austerity apparently took no notice of its demonstrable failings.

Meanwhile, the Harvard economist Alberto Alesina – one of the academics belonging to the Bocconi University in Milan, who had popularized the (also discredited) idea of "expansionary austerity" during the late 1980s – attempted to breathe new life into the "crowding-out" argument in favor of austerity. Reviving the concept of "expansionary fiscal consolidation," he argued that austerity – by restoring the confidence of financial investors – would result in the private sector investing more money than the government withdrew.

In addition, the swift debunking of these ideas would reveal that computer-based data analysis, like the intellectual activity before it, is not always without problems. However, as has so often been the case with arguments about austerity, discrediting the evidence upon which austerity programs have been based has often failed to produce any policy reversals. Nonetheless, it would not be long before one of the principle proponents of post-crash austerity – the International Monetary Fund (IMF) – would indeed begin to openly question its effects.

A Change of Heart at the IMF?

The French economist Olivier Blanchard – chief economist at the IMF from September 2008 to October 2015 – along with other IMF economists, had largely followed the same economic "conventional wisdom" about austerity as Reinhart, Rogoff, Alesina, and others, and had, indeed, actively promoted it.

Following the collapse of Bretton Woods in the early 1970s, its institutions – including the IMF and the World Bank – became strong advocates of neoliberalism. Their new model for providing financial assistance was based on a narrow range of policy instruments, which "stem from classical mainstream economic theory,"[21] with "a strong emphasis on fiscal discipline, including control of inflation, restricting state spending and reducing balance of payments deficits."[22] In response to the Latin American debt crisis, Mexican tequila crisis, East Asian debt crisis, and Turkish, Brazilian, and Russian foreign exchange crises, IMF-designed structural adjustment programs therefore featured austerity and policies designed to increase price flexibility – especially in the labor market.

During the 1990s, however, studies of East Asia's "economic miracle" revealed the central role played by the state. Evidence that World Bank structural adjustment programs had had a negligible effect on growth in Africa also emerged, casting doubt on the IMF's and World Bank's approach. The arrival of the American economist and Nobel Prize winner Joseph Stiglitz as World Bank Chief Economist in 1997 brought a shift in focus – toward economic development and the alleviation of poverty – as the World Bank began to frame its "millennium development goals."

Meanwhile, the IMF continued to demand austerity as a condition for assistance on the grounds that it was thought to be a precondition for both attracting capital and repaying public debts; and in the aftermath of the 2008 financial crisis, these policies were forced upon countries in the global north. The first was Greece, in response to fears of a sovereign debt default. But austerity quickly spread, notably to other countries within Europe, including the UK, as well as – eventually – the United States.

By 2013, however, policymakers and economists at the IMF, as well as the World Bank (but not all politicians), were beginning to accept that austerity was slowing growth and hindering recovery. But they also recognized that, despite having been rescued from melt-down (for which they themselves were largely responsible), the global financial markets were demanding austerity not because of its *economic* effects, but as "credible evidence" that governments were serious about managing their budgets and repaying their debts.

The change of heart didn't stop there. In 2016, the IMF caused a major stir with an article entitled "Neoliberalism: Oversold?" in its journal *Finance and Development*. Focusing on the effects of capital account liberalization and economic austerity policies, the IMF's research revealed:

> Austerity policies not only generate substantial welfare costs due to supply-side channels, they also hurt demand – and thus worsen employment and unemployment … In practice, episodes of fiscal consolidation have been followed, on average, by drops, rather than expansions of output. On average, a consolidation of 1 percent of GDP increases the long-term unemployment rate by 0.6 percentage point and raises by 1.5 percent within 5 years the GINI measure of income inequality."[23]

Thus, unlike Reinhart and Rogoff, who – even after their findings had been discredited – still argued that high public debt levels cause sluggish growth (and austerity is therefore required), the IMF economists were no longer convinced. In the aftermath of the 2008 financial crisis, they concluded that it was actually austerity that was impeding growth, not the other way around – and adding to public debt in the process. They urged policymakers and institutions that advise them to "be guided not by faith, but by evidence of what has worked … [arguing that] countries with ample fiscal space [should be] simply living with high debt and allowing debt ratios to decline organically through growth."[24] But their arguments appear to have fallen on deaf ears.

Conclusions

As we have seen, since the birth of a national debt in its modern form during the late seventeenth century, the evolution of austerity as both an idea and a policy has been closely connected to the role of the state in the economy and society – as well as attitudes towards debt, both public and private. This, in turn, along with their own experience of social, political, and economic events, has influenced theorists' understanding of austerity and its policy applications.

In the next chapter, we will look at the effects of changes in government expenditure and revenues in greater detail, by examining how national accounts work. This will allow us to explore the relationship between a government's deficit and debt – and, hence, the likely impact of austerity and stimulus on an economy. It will also offer insight into how contemporary arguments about austerity stand up. Subsequent chapters will analyze the effects of austerity in different countries, at different times – and under varying social, political, and economic circumstances – to draw out the important political and social dimensions to austerity ideas and policies.

3

National Accounting and the Economics of Austerity

Introduction

As we saw in Chapter 2, economics, politics, and society have evolved out of all recognition since the introduction of a national debt in its modern form during the late seventeenth century. The evolution of public debt – and the uses to which it has been put – were closely interlinked with the industrial revolution and, indeed, the eventual appearance of financialized "postindustrial" economies. Along with the shifting economic role of the state, this also played an important part in the evolution of austerity as both an idea and a policy, with its own economic, political, and social dimensions.

This chapter looks at the two distinct components of a fiscal deficit, as well as considering the relationship between a government's annual fiscal balance and its accumulated public debt. Since both deficits and debt have been much discussed in relation to austerity – with varying degrees of accuracy – it is essential to consider its effect on national accounts. We therefore introduce the idea of "sectoral financial balances" – the relationship between the government's fiscal balance, the domestic private sector balance, and the foreign sector balance – which, by definition, must sum to zero. This means that a change in the financial position of one sector will be accompanied by a change in the others. The sectoral balances framework thus allows us to observe the effect of changes in government spending and taxation on the economy, holding all else constant. We will also explore the fiscal multiplier because, while stimulus and austerity can influence the direction of change in the sectoral balances, the fiscal multiplier will have a significant effect on the size of that change.

Fiscal Deficits and Public Debt

Since there is no precise definition of what austerity actually is, it is unsurprising that significant confusion remains. Nor is it just the public that has a poor understanding of the concept; both politicians and the media frequently – and wrongly – use the terms "deficit" and "debt" interchangeably. In 2013, for example, Britain's then Prime Minister David Cameron was publicly rebuked by the UK Statistics Authority for claiming that, by reducing the fiscal deficit (rather than returning it to surplus), his government was "paying down Britain's debts." At the time, the UK's national debt was in fact rising – which it would, for as long as the budget remained in deficit.

We therefore need to start with what government deficits and public debt actually are, how they relate to each other and, eventually, the sectoral balances framework.

A government's "primary fiscal deficit" (or surplus) is the difference between its annual expenditure and its revenues; its debt includes not only public debt that has been accumulated over previous years, including interest charges, but also the current year's primary deficit. The deficit, however, can be subdivided into two main components: the "cyclical deficit," which is built up during a recession and usually eliminated by a surplus resulting from the subsequent recovery, and the "full employment deficit," which remains relatively consistent across the economic cycle.

Both components are determined by fiscal policy, which can include both "discretionary" and "nondiscretionary" elements. Discretionary fiscal policy requires the government to pass new legislation that explicitly changes tax or spending levels, usually in response to political and economic pressures. Examples include spending on the military, infrastructure projects, and changes in existing taxes. Nondiscretionary fiscal policy involves "automatic stabilizers," which are a commitment to certain types of spending – like unemployment insurance and social welfare benefits – which tend to increase during recessions, when people lose their jobs and/or fall into poverty. Since government revenues from taxes tend to fall during recessions, even as social welfare costs are rising, the cyclical component of the deficit is likely to increase. But when the economy recovers, all of this is reversed: spending on automatic stabilizers naturally falls and tax revenues increase, improving the government's fiscal balance.

Recently – and especially since the turn to austerity following the 2008 financial crisis – government deficits have been viewed as evidence that the government isn't "paying its way." However, if a loan-financed deficit causes the economy to grow in a sustainable way, and the resulting increase in tax and other government revenue grows faster than the deficit, that deficit will eventually disappear. This is because government spending falls into two categories: "current account" spending and "capital account" spending (public investment).

Public finance theory generally suggests that, under the "balanced budget rule," a government should finance current expenditure, which would not generate streams of future tax revenues or other charges, through current tax collection. By contrast, since capital expenditure creates government-owned assets, it is considered acceptable to borrow for such spending, if the assets produced or acquired pay for (or more than pay for) themselves in tax revenues and/or user charges.

Most economists recognize the need for public investment in assets, such as transport, healthcare, and education systems, whose economic benefits spread beyond – and cannot be captured by – any one individual or firm. According to the American economist and Nobel Prize winner Thomas Sargent, "deficits on 'capital account' are justified because they are by definition temporary and the loans undertaken to finance them are 'self-liquidating'."[1]

Sectoral Financial Balances: Accounting for Public Deficits and Debt

The sectoral financial balances framework is an analytical tool that makes it easier to understand the effect of austerity on government accounts, holding other things constant. It brings together both accounting identities derived from the system of national accounts (which measures a country's macroeconomic activity) that are true by definition, and theoretical ideas about relationships between the variables within the accounting structures. This makes it possible to check the logic of political claims about the likely effects of different policies – such as austerity – on the government's sectoral financial balance as well as on other macroeconomic outcomes.

The three sectoral financial balances are: (1) the government's; (2) the domestic private sector's (households and businesses – including banks); and (3) the foreign sector's (households, businesses, and governments). The value of all three can be calculated from the overall value of total spending (GDP) and total income in an economy, through the process of national accounting.

The factors that govern the financial balance in each sector are straightforward enough: the government's fiscal balance is in deficit if spending is higher than revenues from taxation; it is in surplus if tax revenues are higher than public expenditure. The private domestic sector balance is in deficit if it is spending (on investments) more than it is saving; it is in surplus if it is saving more than it is investing (and thus accumulating financial assets). Finally, the foreign sector balance is in deficit if foreigners are spending more on a country's exports than that country is spending on imports; it is in surplus if foreigners are selling more goods and services to the domestic economy than they are purchasing from it.

It is important to note that any deficit must be financed; but this happens in different ways. The government deficit requires budget financing, while the domestic private sector deficit needs private sector investment financing, and the foreign sector deficit necessitates international financing. The government finances its deficit by printing money and/or issuing debt, both of which the private sector is willing to hold because they constitute financial assets. If, at full employment, the private sector continuously builds up savings (because households don't want to spend all their income and firms don't reinvest all their profit), the government must run a deficit in order to absorb private sector savings, unless the country can run a continuous current account surplus and invest those savings abroad.

In any given year, the sectoral financial balances must collectively sum to zero, because the sources of income for the government, domestic private, and foreign sectors (taxes [T], saving [S] and imports [M]) must be exactly equal to their uses (government spending [G], investment [I] and exports [X]). However, that doesn't mean that the individual sectors will be in balance; and, in reality, they almost never are. Rather, in any given year, it means that the surpluses and deficits of the three sectors must balance each other out. Thus, the government deficit is equal to the difference between net domestic private saving and net exports, which is the same as the sum of net private domestic saving and net foreign sector saving.

The foreign sector balance is also termed the "current account," and net foreign sector saving the "capital account." A current account deficit always means an equal and opposite capital account surplus. In other words, the country must be borrowing from abroad or selling assets for foreign currency. This means that a persistent full-employment fiscal deficit may be sustainable even if the government doesn't use all of it to finance public investment.

If the government deficit is financed by foreign capital, with the private sector in balance, both public debt and foreign debt will increase, which can mean trouble for a small open economy. However, this is not a problem for a country like the United States, since use of the dollar as a global reserve currency means a continuous inflow of foreign currency to buy dollars. But if the deficit is financed by private sector saving, external trade can stay balanced and the situation can be sustainable for a long time.

Of course, it is impossible to infer a causal effect from an identity; and, in reality, since sectoral financial balances are causally related by means of changes in national income, to make predictions about the way in which these balances will move requires theories about these relationships and what causes changes in national income. Nevertheless, from a national accounting perspective, in any given year since the three sectoral balances by definition must sum to zero, the sectoral financial balances framework offers a useful way of seeing how a change in the government's deficit (or surplus) can be expected to impact both the nongovernmental sector balance and GDP.

The Sectoral Financial Balances Model of Aggregate Demand

The sectoral financial balances model of aggregate demand[2] relates the desired government financial balance with the desired nongovernmental financial balance, illustrating the relationship between the government's budget deficit (or surplus), the nongovernmental sector financial balance and GDP. We therefore use it to create a graphical representation of a country's financial flows in order to understand changes in both the financial status of the various sectors of the economy and the effect that a change in discretionary fiscal policy – such as austerity – is likely to have on the sectoral financial balances and overall economic performance.

In constructing the graphical representation of the sectoral balances, we will consider the nongovernmental sector surplus curve and the government sector deficit curve separately, before putting them together to assess the likely effect of discretionary changes in fiscal policy (holding all else constant).

Graph 1 shows the nongovernmental sector surplus curve (NG[+]1). The vertical axis represents the sectoral financial balances, and the horizontal axis represents GDP. As we discussed above, a public sector deficit is, by definition, equal to a nongovernmental sector surplus; and a public sector surplus is equal to a nongovernmental sector deficit. Hence, on the vertical axis, positive values (above the horizontal axis) represent the public sector deficit and nongovernmental sector surplus, and negative values (below the horizontal axis) represent the public sector surplus and nongovernmental sector deficit.

The NG[+]1 curve represents the desired total net saving of the combined nongovernmental sector. It is upward sloping because higher levels of GDP correspond to higher incomes; income is also positively related to both saving and imports. So at higher levels of GDP, both saving and imports will also be higher, and at lower levels of GDP, they will be lower.

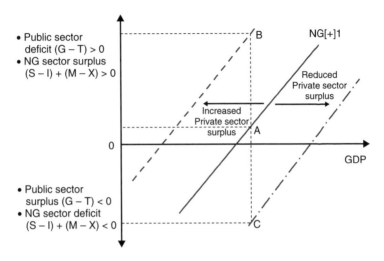

Graph 1 The nongovernmental sector surplus curve

Shifts in the curve are the result of efforts to restructure nongovernmental sector balance sheets, through changes in saving relative to investment and/or imports relative to exports. If nongovernmental sector financial balances include high levels of debt, for example, de-leveraging will shift the curve to the left; and at any level of GDP, the nongovernmental sector surplus will be higher (as shown by the difference between point A on NG[+]1 and point B). On the other hand, a drop in saving relative to investment and/or imports relative to exports will shift the curve to the right – and the nongovernmental sector surplus will be lower (as shown by the difference between point A on NG[+]1 and point C).

The government deficit curve (G[–]1) is illustrated in Graph 2. The G[–]1 curve slopes downward, because at higher levels of GDP, tax revenues tend to be higher and spending on automatic stabilizers lower, with a correspondingly lower fiscal deficit. At lower levels of GDP, though, tax revenues tend to be lower and spending on automatic stabilizers higher; with a correspondingly higher government deficit.

Shifts in the curve are caused by discretionary changes in government spending and/or taxes. Austerity (a decrease in government spending and/or increase in taxes) will shift the

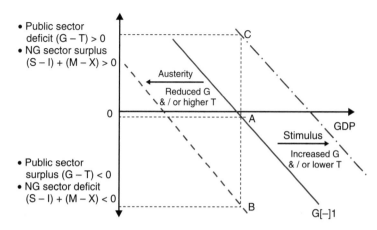

Graph 2 The government deficit curve

curve to the left and the government deficit will be lower (shown by the difference between point A on G[–]1 and point B). By contrast, economic stimulus measures (an increase in government spending and/or decrease in taxes) will shift the curve to the right; and the government sector deficit will be higher (shown by the difference between point A on G[–]1 and point C).

The two curves are brought together in Graph 3. The full employment level of GDP (GDP$_{FE}$) is also specified. The "equilibrium" – or "intra-sectoral balance" – point is where NG[+]1 and G[–]1 cross. This is where the public and private sectors are individually in balance. The intra-sectoral balance point is at GDP1, which is below the full employment level of GDP, and there is a public sector and nongovernmental sector balance of zero. As this happens below full-employment GDP, it doesn't have any of the desirable properties of "equilibrium." There is therefore nothing virtuous about balancing the budget if the private sector is looking for a safe way to invest net saving (which public debt can provide). In any case, the private sector can be in overall balance with a large excess (or shortage) of saving being offset by a significant outflow (or inflow) of capital, neither of which is likely to be sustainable.

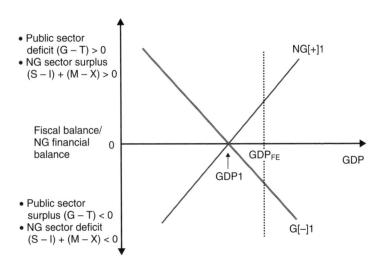

Graph 3 Sectoral financial balances

From this starting point, we can now consider the effect of a change in fiscal policy on both GDP and the government and nongovernmental sector balances.

The effect of economic stimulus

Returning to Graph 3, although the public and nongovernmental sector financial accounts are in balance, the economy is operating at a level of GDP that is below full employment, which usually means excess capacity, as well as underemployed resources. In response, the government could attempt to move the economy closer to full employment, through economic stimulus. This would cause the government deficit curve to shift upward and to the right.

This is illustrated in Graph 4, with the shift from G[–]1 to G[–]2. All else is held constant, including the nongovernmental surplus curve. In this illustration, the government is successful in reaching its target of a full employment level of GDP. The result is an increase in GDP, from GDP1 to GDP$_{FE}$, and an increase in both the public sector deficit and private sector surplus, from zero to G-deficit/NG-surplus1.

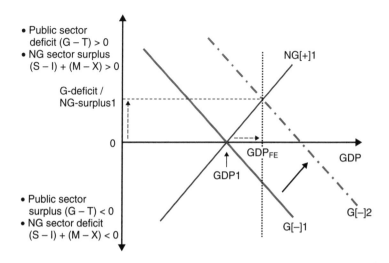

Graph 4 Sectoral financial balances and economic stimulus

The effect of economic austerity

In Graph 4, at GDP$_{FE}$, although the economy is at full employment – above which there is a risk of overheating – the government budget is in deficit. Thus, to reduce the deficit (and accumulated public debt), as well as avert the risk of inflation and financial crisis, the government could decide to implement austerity measures.

In Graph 5, this is illustrated by a shift from G[–]2 to G[–]3, with everything else held constant. The result is an improvement in the government's fiscal position, but with a deterioration in the private sector balance, from G-deficit/NG-surplus1 to G-deficit/NG-surplus2, and a reduction in GDP, from GDP$_{FE}$ to GDP2.

At GDP2, since the economy is now at less than full employment, there are unemployed and underemployed resources; and although the government financial balance has improved, it is still in deficit – which means that the government's debt level is continuing to rise.

Thus, Graph 5 shows a simplified illustration of the situation faced by many countries following the 2008 financial crisis. Having bailed out banks and implemented massive

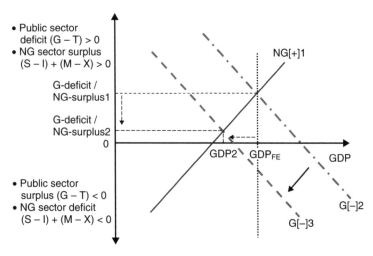

Graph 5 Sectoral financial balances and austerity

emergency stimulus measures, the resulting fiscal deficits and high public debt levels raised concerns about the risk of sovereign debt default, first in the Eurozone and then elsewhere. In 2010, this caused a general turn to austerity. Although some countries were successful in reducing their deficits – albeit not eliminating them – public debt levels continued to rise. So despite the clear illustration above, of why this was inevitable – and ignoring both economic stagnation and high unemployment – many countries imposed ever more austerity.

The effect of austerity following the 2008 crisis

Graph 5 could be brought even closer to the situation experienced during the 2008 financial crisis if we also show the effect of a shift of the nongovernmental surplus curve to the left, as shown in Graph 6.

The sharp decline in asset prices during the crisis damaged the private sector's balance sheets and forced it to rebuild them by pushing saving a long way above investment. At the

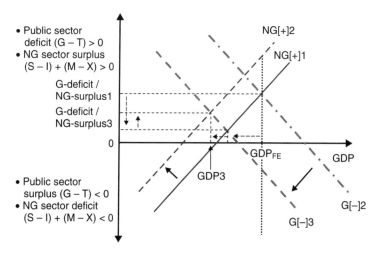

Graph 6 A more realistic graphical illustration of the 2008 financial crisis

same time, the recession caused a fall in exports. So to achieve the necessary surplus of exports over imports (for the overall private sector balance), a lower level of imports was required. In turn, this meant lower GDP, so the budget deficit problems described above are more realistically shown to be the result of the combined effect of a leftward shift in both the government deficit (G[–]) and the nongovernmental surplus (NG[+]) curves.

The result will of course be an even lower level of GDP (GDP3) and a higher government deficit/nongovernmental sector surplus (G-deficit/NG-surplus3) For austerity to contribute to a reduction in public debt, the government financial balance would need to be in surplus. In Graph 6, this would require the government deficit curve to shift far enough to the left, to intersect with the nongovernmental surplus curve below the zero point, putting the government budget into surplus, where it would need to remain for some time to reduce public debt.

So what are the implications for the sustainability of the private sector financial situation after 2008 – and has austerity policy helped or hindered progress?

The crisis moved saving above investment. By investing much less (relative to saving), private sector agents hoped to rebuild their balance sheets. This would have been possible, without any change in the public sector balance, if the drop in private expenditure had pulled imports a long way below exports. But imports include many essentials (like food and energy) that are hard to economize on, and exports were held down by the simultaneous drop in international trading partners' incomes. So the private sector could only achieve its additional net saving by running a higher overall surplus. As we have seen, this automatically requires the public sector to run a higher deficit. Had governments tried to rein in a deficit immediately, there would be no way that saving could rise in relation to investment, until a world recovery started to raise exports relative to imports.

As we will see in the case studies, some countries did manage to "escape" this situation. This was the result of a number of factors. First, many people sacrificed consumption – even of basic items – causing a reduction in imports. Households also started borrowing again, so saving didn't rise relative to investment, interrupting repair of the domestic private sector balance sheet. Third, seeing the damage caused by austerity, governments outside of the Eurozone eased off on deficit reduction.

But despite this, austerity may well not be sustainable for countries that entered the recession with large external deficits and imposed austerity early. In some of these cases, although deficits are gradually coming down, the corresponding "rebalancing" of the private sector includes sharply rising household debt – with mortgage-financed house purchases being included in investment. At the same time, there has been a worsening foreign imbalance, mainly financed by the sale of assets to overseas investors. The private and external sectors are therefore running down assets and building up debts, as an inevitable result of governments starting to pay off their debt.

In this context, austerity cannot be expected to reduce public debt, since any improvement in the public deficit is likely to be too slow and too small to make a material impact on the stock of government debt; and any gains in the public deficit are being offset by a deterioration in private and overseas financial balances. By contrast, a significant expansionary agenda could work to the advantage of private and overseas – as well as public – financial balances.

The graphical analysis helps in understanding the direction of change in both the government and nongovernmental sectoral financial balances and GDP. However, the actual changes will depend partly on the scale of the stimulus or austerity program and partly on the size of the fiscal multiplier, which we'll explore in the next section. It will similarly depend upon the marginal propensities to consume, save, import, and tax, which will also help determine the slopes of the sectoral financial balances curves. But these are beyond the scope of the graphical representation here.

Double or Quits: The Fiscal Multiplier

As we have seen, while changes in fiscal policy will influence the direction of GDP growth through their effect on a country's sectoral financial balances, the magnitude of the effect will be significantly affected by the size of the fiscal multiplier, as will the success of a policy of fiscal austerity or stimulus.

The fiscal multiplier is the ratio of the change in GDP, given a unit change in government spending. For example, if the fiscal multiplier is 0.5 – as the IMF believed it was in 2010, when austerity was introduced in many countries – a one unit decrease in government spending should cause a decrease in GDP of 0.5 units. On the other hand, a one unit *increase* in government spending should produce an increase in GDP of 0.5 units. Thus, the smaller the fiscal multiplier, the less a program of austerity is likely to stress an economy. A larger multiplier however, will push an economy more sharply towards recession – or deeper into it.

In 2012, however, new IMF research suggested that, from the start of the world recession in 2008, fiscal multipliers were actually much larger than 0.5 – and in the range of 0.9 to 1.7[3] – a finding that was consistent with earlier research. If this is in fact true – and especially if a country's fiscal multiplier is well above 1 – austerity is not only unlikely to achieve its objective of reducing the government's fiscal deficit, but its effect on overall economic performance will be seriously damaging.

In short, if the fiscal multiplier is positive but less than 1, austerity will cause GDP to fall by less than the reduction in government spending; and stimulus will cause it to rise by less than the spending increase. On the other hand, if the multiplier is positive and greater than 1, austerity will cause GDP to fall by more than the public spending cut, thereby reinforcing recession; stimulus, on the other hand, will cause it to rise by more than the increase in spending. However, the fiscal multiplier could, in theory at least, also be negative, if, for example, a rising government deficit causes a sharp reduction in confidence. In this case, austerity could cause GDP to increase, while stimulus might lead to a reduction in GDP. This was part of the rationale in support of the turn to austerity in 2010.

Despite the fiscal multiplier's effect being technically straightforward to calculate, it is very difficult to measure – and even harder to predict. It varies both between countries and in different economic contexts. In a large country such as the United States, for example, where an increase in government spending is likely to be met by domestic production, the multiplier will be relatively large. In smaller open economies, however, like Iceland or Ireland, where extra government spending will be primarily met with supplies originating elsewhere, it will be smaller. Thus, a country's economic structure – what is produced at home, as opposed to what is imported – and the nature of its trade regime will have an influence on the size of its fiscal multiplier.

The current state of the economy also influences the size of the fiscal multiplier. If a country is in recession and unemployment is high, it will be relatively large, since any increase in demand generated by government spending will be met with an increase in supply, boosting employment to produce the goods and services required. If an economy is at close to full employment, though, the fiscal multiplier will be very low, with any increase in government spending being likely to displace private sector spending.

The size of the fiscal multiplier will also be a function of the form taken by fiscal policy. Spending on the direct production of newly produced, labor-intensive goods and services, or on transfer programs for the unemployed, will be associated with relatively high fiscal multipliers. This is because new goods and services will create new jobs. Since those at the lower end of the distribution of income and wealth tend to spend a higher proportion of what they receive than the more affluent, the impact of fiscal policy supporting more economically vulnerable groups will have a relatively strong impact on GDP. By contrast, the fiscal multiplier will be quite small for transfers and subsidies such as tax cuts or rebates going to the relatively better-off, or to corporations. This is because recipients are mostly on a higher income with a higher propensity to save; so this is the logic of the balanced budget multiplier in reverse.

Yet another factor influencing the fiscal multiplier is whether austerity is likely to be short term or sustained, with short-term measures having relatively small effects on the economy. It will also be influenced by the policy responses of others, including the Central Bank and the governments of other countries. For example, in an environment where monetary policy is constrained by the zero lower bound on interest rates (if Central Bank interest rates are close to zero) – as it has been since the 2008 financial crisis – and where numerous countries are pursuing austerity at the same time, the fiscal multiplier will again be relatively high.

Conclusions

As we have seen, while the effect of austerity might be an improvement in the government's fiscal deficit, it will not necessarily result in a reduction in public debt. This is because reducing public debt will only happen if the austerity program is able to generate a sustained fiscal surplus, which itself will depend upon the private sector being able to increase its net exports in line with its net saving (not a likely scenario when major trading partners are also in recession). Austerity is also likely to negatively impact both the nongovernmental financial balance and GDP. Only if the economy is operating at a level close to full employment will a policy of austerity be appropriate, reducing the risk of inflation and financial crisis.

Either way, the actual impact of austerity will depend upon the scale of the fiscal consolidation, the marginal propensities to consume, save, tax, and import and (for a small open economy) the sensitivity of exports to the national price level and foreign countries' income – and the size of the notoriously hard to predict fiscal multiplier.

With these ideas in mind, the next chapter lays out the arguments that have been marshaled to justify austerity, along with their implications for policy and outcomes.

4

Selling Austerity: Economics, Politics, and Society

Introduction

Chapter 3 clearly demonstrates that, from a technical point of view, austerity makes the economy worse off in terms of GDP, particularly when the economy is in recession. So if the economy is already in bad shape – as it has been in many countries since the 2008 financial crisis – why would a government pursue such a policy?

In some cases, such as the Eurozone, where individual countries do not have control over their currency, austerity was imposed as a condition for financial support. In others – such as the United States and the United Kingdom – which not only have control over their currency but also have a floating exchange rate and therefore the option of devaluation to make their exports more attractive, austerity was a deliberate policy choice, but motivated by politics, rather than economics. These cases and others will be examined in more detail in Chapters 5 through 8, which explore the political, social, and cultural – as well as economic – dimensions of austerity.

In this chapter, we will assess some of the arguments that have recently been marshaled in support of austerity, many of which have roots in the much earlier debates discussed in Chapter 2. We will also have a closer look at a key measure used to gauge a country's level of indebtedness – the public debt-to-GDP ratio – to see whether, on its own, it can be used to justify austerity.

Does the Public Debt-to-GDP Ratio Tell You When It's Time for Austerity?

The development of economics at a time when many advances were being made in the pure sciences suggested to early economists that their own field might also be governed by such immutable laws as those that applied in chemistry or physics – an idea that has never entirely gone away. There have even been attempts to define specific laws for austerity. One of the most influential of these is the effort to identify a level of government debt at which GDP growth is inhibited, using the debt-to-GDP ratio.

The public debt-to-GDP ratio measures a country's sovereign debt as a proportion of its GDP. Since shifts in *both* public debt *and* GDP can influence the public debt-to-GDP ratio, it is useful to consider the effect of changes in public debt (the numerator) and GDP (the denominator) on the public debt-to-GDP ratio.

The ratio can be expected to increase, even if GDP is growing, when the rise in public debt is greater than GDP growth; it will also increase if both public debt and GDP are falling, but GDP is falling faster than debt, or when there is no change in public debt but GDP is contracting. The public debt-to-GDP ratio will be stable if the change in public debt is matched by the change in GDP. The public debt-to-GDP ratio will fall only when: (1) GDP is increasing at the same time as public debt is being reduced; (2) GDP is not changing but public debt is being reduced; or (3) both GDP and public debt are falling, but debt is falling faster than GDP.

Much has been made of the public debt-to-GDP ratio by politicians, financiers, and media alike. However, while it provides a basic snapshot of an economy's debt position, there are a number of significant factors that are not included in the equation. Nevertheless, by comparing what a country owes to what it produces, the public debt-to-GDP ratio is seen by some to be an indicator of a government's ability to repay its debt; and higher public debt-to-GDP ratios may lead investors to demand a higher rate of interest to compensate for any extra perceived risk of default. This, in turn, could add to the government's fiscal deficit, potentially setting off a vicious cycle of increasing public debt and interest charges.

However, the public debt-to-GDP ratio is not necessarily a good predictor of whether a country is likely to default. This will also depend upon who holds the government's debt, as well as whether the country has control over its currency. In 2017, for example, Japan's debt-to-GDP ratio was the highest in the world, at around 240 percent. But Japan was in no danger of default because the debt was mostly held by its own citizens; and since Japan has control over its currency, it can both issue debt in that currency and print more to pay it off. By contrast, if a high proportion of a country's sovereign debt is held by potentially hostile foreign investors, banks, and governments – and if the country does not have control over its currency, as is the case for member countries of the Eurozone – a high public debt-to-GDP ratio can be a serious problem. This is a large part of the reason that Greece and other heavily indebted Eurozone countries were required to impose austerity in return for financial assistance from the Troika (the International Monetary Fund (IMF), European Central Bank, and European Commission).

The public debt-to-GDP ratio can also show whether an economy is in a recession or recovery. An increasing public debt-to-GDP ratio often signals a recession, when GDP contracts, tax revenues fall, and government spending on automatic stabilizers rises – increasing the cyclical component of the fiscal deficit and overall public debt. During a recovery, the public debt-to-GDP ratio typically falls as GDP rises, boosting tax revenues, easing spending on welfare, and reducing the cyclical component of the fiscal deficit, which in turn relieves pressure on public debt levels.

Because of these factors, it is better to view the public debt-to-GDP ratio as part of a trend, not a single snapshot. Although much of the justification for austerity following the 2008 crisis rested on high levels of public debt, the recession following the crisis would automatically worsen the public debt-to-GDP ratio anyway – so it should have caused little alarm.

The public debt-to-GDP ratio can be an influential policy tool; and it played a significant (if misguided) role in the general turn to austerity following the 2008 financial crisis – but for *political* rather than *economic* reasons. This strongly suggests that before coming to any practical overall assessment, it is necessary to separate the political, social, and cultural aspects of austerity from its economic dimensions. We will do this in more depth in Chapters 5 through 8, using key cases where austerity has been implemented – for various reasons – since the turbulent interwar years.

Political and cultural dimensions, though, are not limited to the policy of austerity alone; they also feature strongly in some of the arguments that have been used to support it.

The Debate over Austerity

Arguments about the acceptable level of public debt have continued, more or less uninterrupted, for three hundred years or so. Most of the original arguments for government debt reduction (austerity) first appeared at a time when the money was mostly used for wars, there was no state-run welfare program, very few people could vote, and taxes were levied largely on consumption and property. This meant that debt was usually regarded as temporary and could be eliminated without much complication – and there was no need to convince a potentially hostile electorate that doing so was a good idea. This is also when the idea of "crowding-out" first appeared – an idea that cast the state as an unhelpful competitor in the nascent (and limited) financial markets – and when government accounts were compared with those of a household or business – which at that point was largely true.

However, burgeoning credit flows in ever-expanding financial markets have removed much of the foundation for the "crowding-out" argument, while changes to tax systems and the introduction of welfare state spending have undermined the comparison between state and business or household budgets. Meanwhile, during the interwar years, Keynes considered these changed circumstances and developed a new theory of the economy in his *General Theory of Employment, Interest and Money*. He argued that state spending – and hence austerity – both have a key role to play. But austerity was much harder to sell than government spending, especially with universal suffrage now playing a part.

Nevertheless, all these ideas do have one thing in common. Against the odds, they're all still being made today – which suggests that many of them, at least, have an emotional or political, rather than a technical, economic basis. They are therefore worthy of consideration in some detail.

"Crowding-out"

"Crowding-out" is one argument that has long been used to justify economic austerity, taking the view that government deficit spending, whether financed by taxes or borrowing, diverts resources from the private sector. From this perspective, when a government borrows money in the money market, it is seen as competing with private investors for a limited volume of credit – causing the interest rate to rise. Since private investors might be expected to borrow less at higher rates, fewer private investments will then be made; so government borrowing is said to "crowd-out" some amount of potential private investment.

The American economist John Cochrane sums it up like this: "Every dollar of increased government spending must correspond to one less dollar of private spending. Jobs created by stimulus spending are offset by jobs lost from the decline in private spending. We can build roads instead of factories but fiscal stimulus can't help build more of both."[1]

This is similar to the argument made by the American economist and Nobel Prize winner Milton Friedman (1912–2006) during the 1960s – that government spending, even on public goods like libraries and schools, displaces private sector alternatives. According to this logic, state spending prevents private investors from spending on such things, with the government's spending being counteracted by a decrease in private spending, producing no net benefit for the economy. Thus, instead of increasing aggregate demand, government spending merely changes the mix between government and private investment. Friedman then goes on to suggest that the only situation in which government spending would have a positive impact on aggregate demand would be if it created something useless – with no viable private sector alternative.

Those opposed to this argument admit that some government spending can be wasteful – especially if it is indeed spent on useless items. However, they also point out the benefits of creating jobs for such people as public school and university teachers, firefighters, and police men and women in order to protect the public, and construction workers so as to build public infrastructure. Rather than displacing private investment, these initiatives often encourage more of it.

Another variant of the "crowding-out" hypothesis is the idea of "expansionary austerity" – where fiscal consolidation is seen to improve GDP growth. This idea takes two different but complementary forms: so-called "Ricardian equivalence," which is discussed in the section below on "psychological crowding-out," and the idea that government deficit spending absorbs private sector saving that could otherwise fund private investment.

According to the American economist Eugene Fama, "stimulus plans absorb saving that would otherwise go to private investment ... Stimulus spending must be financed, which means it displaces other current uses of the same funds."[2] This draws upon the sectoral balances framework discussed above. If we are considering the world economy as a whole, the foreign sector disappears; and total private investment (I) is equal to the sum of private sector saving (S) and government saving (T – G). To finance deficit spending (government dis-saving), governments issue more sovereign debt, which is seen to absorb private sector saving that would otherwise be available to fund private investment, causing it to fall by the same amount by which the government deficit goes up.

From this perspective, government spending simply moves resources from one use to another. So economic stimulus will only benefit the economy if public funds are spent on activities that are more productive than the private investments they displace. While conceding that some government investments are in principle productive – particularly those with widespread positive spillovers ("externalities"), such as major transport systems – proponents of this view argue that, unlike private sector investments, state spending is prone to inefficiency.

Since the "investment equals saving" equation holds for the global economy but not necessarily for an individual national economy, if the extra sovereign debt issued to finance a government's deficit spending is purchased by foreigners, additional government spending can be made without a corresponding reduction in private spending. However, supporters argue that, at a future date, those foreigners can be expected to take back their resources, plus interest. Also, if public spending generates less wealth than it cost, the loss is borne by future taxpayers, when the government debt is repaid.

A related viewpoint is that an increase in deficit spending, and the subsequent rise in public debt, puts a heavy tax burden on future generations, to service the debt. Critics of this perspective do not disagree that a national debt transfers money from taxpayers to bondholders, or that an increase in the ratio of interest payments to GDP should not be allowed to continue forever. But deficit spending to alleviate serious short-term economic difficulties should not be subordinated to the long-term objective of paying down a country's public debt and reducing interest payments on that debt. From this perspective, the best way to lower the national debt is to have a strong economy with extended periods of low unemployment, generating sufficient tax revenue to reduce the public debt-to-GDP ratio and keep deficits at manageable levels if not generating a surplus.

Critics of the "crowding-out" hypothesis argue that there might be some truth in it – but only when the economy is operating at full employment; so, when the government spends more money, it competes with private businesses for employees and resources, resulting in higher wage rates and higher interest rates, which in turn result in reduced private investment spending.

This is effectively an argument in favor of countercyclical austerity during a boom, since, during a recession, with unemployed labor and businesses operating below full capacity, regardless of the interest rate, firms will be reluctant to borrow and invest until they feel confident that demand will be sufficient to provide a satisfactory return on their investment. Government deficit spending, then, has the potential to generate a "crowding-in" process, by helping to increase incomes and spending, in turn adding to the higher demand caused by government spending. Businesses, seeing this economic activity, will become more optimistic and increase investment, thereby supporting recovery and allowing the government to step back as the private sector starts to drive the expansion.

"Psychological crowding-out"

The globalization and deregulation of finance – especially the removal of capital movement restrictions following the collapse of the Bretton Woods system during the 1970s – has long since increased the supply of available credit to a point where most of the original "crowding-out" arguments above are now very difficult to sustain – except perhaps through sheer force of habit. However, there have also been a few new and intriguing variants.

"Psychological crowding-out" focuses on the impact of deficits on confidence and/or expectations about the future and emerged from the Victorian theory of fiscal policy, in which the state's credit-worthiness depends upon a balanced budget. According to this logic, deficits and accumulated public debt undermine confidence in the government's ability to manage the economy and repay its debts. Thus, an increase in government spending – especially if financed by borrowing – would be expected to reduce private investment, with damaging effects on GDP growth. By contrast, austerity should have a positive effect on business expectations, "crowding-in" private sector spending. Some economists, such as Alberto Alesina and Francesco Giavazzi – both associated with the Bocconi University in Milan, where this idea was popularized during the 1980s (and ultimately discredited) – argue that cutting spending is preferable to raising taxes, since higher taxes are more likely to lower investors' confidence.

A variant of this is the idea of "Ricardian equivalence." David Ricardo was himself skeptical about the practical relevance of his idea of "equivalence," which assumes that consumer and business decisions are based on (rational) expectations about the future, however uncertain that might be. Nevertheless, he argued that, in response to deficit spending, forward-looking taxpayers will anticipate higher future taxes to repay the resulting debt – and reduce spending to accumulate the savings required to cover the expected increase in taxation.

Thus, when public deficits and indebtedness are high, private sector spending is assumed to be weak because households and firms increase saving in anticipation of future tax increases. Conversely, so the "expansionary austerity" story goes, if governments cut – or promise to cut – spending and reduce fiscal deficits, private sector prospects will improve due to an anticipated reduction in future taxes. This is assumed to cause saving to fall and private sector consumption and investment to rise, offsetting the decrease in public spending and increasing GDP growth.

Yet another strand of the "psychological crowding-out" hypothesis focuses on sovereign bond investors' confidence, arguing that the real effect of a bond-financed stimulus package is higher interest rates – not caused by a shortage of saving, but by a lack of confidence in the government's stimulus program and hence its reliability in servicing its debt. Investors will thus demand higher returns to compensate for the perceived higher risk. It is therefore argued that a major reduction in government spending – or a plan to reduce deficits and retire public debts – is likely to have the opposite effect, and will help reduce interest charges on a country's national debt.

Opponents of this idea instead argue that the evidence simply doesn't bear it out, since countries with very high fiscal deficits and public debt-to-GDP ratios – such as the USA, Japan, and the UK – are paying lower rates of interest on their public debt than those with much lower levels of fiscal deficits and sovereign debt. To explain this, they argue that confidence tracks the performance of the *economy*, rather than the government fiscal balance; so austerity – by undermining growth – also undermines confidence.

Likening a government budget to that of a household or business

Confidence, then, has less to do with economics than with beliefs that may or may not be justified. One of the oldest and most enduring of these is the analogy made between a government budget and that of a household or business – and the idea that it therefore requires balancing.

More than four hundred years ago, the Anglo-Dutch political economist, philosopher, and satirist Bernard de Mandeville (1690–1733), in *The Fable of the Bees: Or, Private Vices, Publick Benefits*, began with an indictment of the extravagance of the rich ruling class of the day – and the hypocrisy of their making a "virtue" out of austerity and thrift (of everyone else). However, when a prosperous society (of bees) decided to stop all excess spending, the hive collapsed. De Mandeville was making the point that the spending of the wealthy had the public benefit of providing a source of livelihood for others. This was controversial because not only did it suggest that individual virtue (austerity) could be a public vice; it also implied that excessive spending could have a public benefit. De Mandeville was describing the "fallacy of composition" – the idea that what is true of the parts may not be true of the whole – which Keynes would return to some two hundred years later. From this perspective, while individual austerity was generally assumed to be good for society, collective austerity may have the opposite effect.

As we saw in Chapter 2, the classical political economists, like Adam Smith and Jean-Baptiste Say, likened a government budget to that of a household or business – and at the time, this made economic sense. However, with the introduction of modern "economic stabilizers" – especially following World War I – government accounts started to behave in very different ways from those of the average household or business, with some unpleasant and apparently intractable economic results.

As a result, when Keynes was theorizing, the economy – and the role of the state within it – differed considerably from that facing earlier economists. In *The General Theory*, Keynes explained the fallacy of composition inherent in drawing the analogy between a government budget and that of a private household or business: while it may be true that over the long term individual firms and households cannot spend more than they earn, in the economy as a whole, people earn what they and others spend. If spending falls short, earnings are lost; and, as a result, labor and other economic resources become unemployed. This has a negative multiplier effect, further reducing income, effective demand, and employment. Because labor and capital are not immediately mobile, such adjustments can be slow and painful, so that unemployed and underemployed labor and other productive resources can be wasted for extended periods of time.

However, in spite of this, nearly a century later, following the 2008 financial crisis, politicians and the media still likened a government budget to that of a household or business, calling for reductions in public spending to balance the government's budget and pay off its debt. In 2010, for example, in a speech proposing a freeze on federal employee pay, then President Barack Obama, said: "After all, small businesses and families are tightening their belts ... Their government should, too."[3]

However, as we saw in Chapter 3, analysis of the workings of sectoral financial balances and the fiscal multiplier clearly demonstrate a number of fundamental flaws in this comparison. It is also misleading to suggest that when public deficits and debts are high – analogous to when households and firms have accumulated too much debt – it is necessary to "stop living above one's means," to "tighten one's belt" and suffer the "pain" of austerity to eliminate them, with anything less being portrayed as fiscally irresponsible.

Unlike a household or firm, a sovereign state that issues its own currency and has a floating exchange rate is not operationally constrained by its budget as it can both issue and adjust the value of its currency to manage a deficit. Likewise, while a household or firm can balance its budget by reducing spending and repaying its debts, without undesirable side effects, a government cannot; during a slump, government deficits inevitably rise due to falling tax revenues and rising unemployment-related social costs, increasing public debt, while GDP growth slows. Cutting public spending won't just deepen the slump; it will also increase public debt.

Keynes – and the timing of austerity

The so-called "Keynesian" argument in relation to government austerity and stimulus is often misrepresented as being biased toward stimulus. During the late 1920s and 1930s, Keynes was accused of ignoring the need to maintain confidence in both the authorities' financial policies and Britain's position in the international community. This ignored the fact that, in his analysis, austerity was indeed vital – but during the boom, in order to curb inflation or the risk of financial collapse, not to further slow an already sluggish economy.

Nonetheless, Keynes recognized the difficulties associated with selling the idea of austerity during a boom, since both politicians and voters would be more likely to favor tax cuts to spending cuts. Nevertheless, in 1937, in a series of articles in *The Times*, he argued that the time for austerity had come, "to protect us from the excesses of the boom and, at the same time, put us in good trim to ward off the cumulative dangers of the slump when the reaction comes, as come it surely will." He also famously wrote: "The boom, not the slump, is the right time for austerity at the Treasury." Keynes thus made explicit the point that while during the slump the cure for unemployment is stimulus, once a recovery is established, austerity is required both to prevent the economy from over-heating and triggering inflationary pressures as well as to provide headroom for the next stimulus.

From Keynes's perspective, then, the choice between stimulus and austerity depends entirely upon the state of the economy. When the economy is at full employment, additional public expenditure will probably "crowd-out" real resources, so austerity will help avoid overheating and inflation. But when the economy's resources are underemployed, a deficit from fiscal stimulus is not deferred taxation but a boost to economic activity until a recovery is sufficiently well established to encourage the private sector to take over in driving it.

Conclusions

The debate over austerity has a long history; and it is wide-ranging and vociferous, with valid arguments on both sides. The real question though, is not so much whether austerity is a "good" or a "bad" economic policy, so much as whether austerity is an *appropriate* policy for a given economic context.

As we have seen, a variety of hypotheses in favor of economic austerity have been put forward, particularly since 2010, when investors became concerned about the high levels of sovereign debt that many developed countries had accumulated. Most relate to the notion of "crowding-out" – both economically and psychologically. This has focused attention on austerity in response to potential problems arising from high levels of public debt – but regardless of context. Only one argument in favor of austerity – the "Keynesian" one – considers the question of which economic circumstances might necessitate such a policy.

We have also seen that the arguments about austerity have not been limited to purely economic factors, with political, social, and cultural influences featuring in many – if not most – cases. To explore the influence of these relatively "soft" factors, and to evaluate the part that austerity has played in a variety of different circumstances, in Chapters 5 through 8, we examine a selection of key case studies in which austerity has been implemented – either voluntarily or as a condition for financial assistance – and the social, political, and economic outcomes that have been realized.

5
Austerity and Welfare: An Unstable Mixture. Britain, Germany, and America between the Wars

Introduction

Following the 2008 financial crisis, the debate about the effect of austerity on economic growth has been highly polarized. One side argues that austerity is expansionary when achieved through spending cuts rather than higher taxes – while the other contends that fiscal consolidation of any sort is harmful to growth when implemented during a recession. What is usually overlooked is the *actual* experience of countries that have pursued fiscal austerity and those that chose an alternative strategy – and whether or not the outcomes matched expectations. The next four chapters will factor this into the debate.

This chapter examines the cases of Great Britain, Germany, and the United States during the turbulent interwar years. What becomes clear is that the timing of austerity is crucial. Get it right, and debt can be reduced; get it wrong, and it is likely not only to cause economic damage but also to provoke social and labor unrest and political instability.

Austerity in Interwar Britain: The "Treasury View"

Although Britain had won World War I, the costs had been enormous; and the economy soon entered a deep depression. In 1920, Lloyd George's Liberal government, assuming that the rise in unemployment would be temporary, set up an Unemployment Grants Committee to encourage public works. However, the costs involved raised doubts about the government's ability to service the 1917 war loan and retain the confidence of its creditors, encouraging a deflationary bias in government policy.

In 1922, Stanley Baldwin, the Conservative Chancellor, warned that "money taken for government purposes is money taken away from trade, and borrowing will thus tend to depress trade and increase unemployment."[1] The justification for this "Treasury View" was provided by Ralph Hawtrey, the Treasury's economist, who argued that "[t]he original contention that the public works themselves give additional employment is radically fallacious. When employment is improved, this is the result of some reaction on credit, and the true remedy for unemployment is to be found in a direct regulation of credit on sound lines."[2] In other words, he thought that the level of saving determines investment – and monetary policy would effectively counter economic fluctuations.

This view was contested by John Maynard Keynes, who argued that the solution to Britain's economic problems lay in increasing home demand to compensate for shrinking export markets. In his view, until the private sector had the confidence to undertake employment-generating investments, there was a role for government investment, to fill the gap between the actual and full-employment levels of effective demand.

Policy aims

This was not the first time Britain had experienced these circumstances. The end of the Napoleonic Wars in 1815 had also brought a major slump – and a national debt that made the 1917 war loan seem relatively affordable. Some, including the political economist Thomas Malthus, attributed that slump to under-consumption following the wars' end. Policy aims, too, were similar, with the reduction of public debt and maintaining confidence in the currency being top of the list. Both aims were eventually achieved, as a result of strong economic growth with progression of the industrial revolution. However, high levels of taxation and unemployment, accompanying the re-entry into the labor market of those returning from war, led to industrial unrest, political organization, and calls for better representation.

But not everything was the same. The government now had ongoing commitments to social welfare – not something to be abandoned lightly, particularly given the all-too-recent 1917 Russian revolution. This meant that, for the first time, government costs went up during a recession. But this was only half the problem, as the British government was now increasingly reliant on income tax for its revenue. Unlike the previous system, based on property and consumption, income tax revenues tended to fall sharply during recessions. Thus, while it might have been possible to manage the state's budget in a more similar manner to that of a business or household in the past, those days were gone.

It would, however, take time, much debate, and considerable economic pain before ideas about the new dynamics of government budgets and debt, taking account of the changed circumstances, would emerge – and yet more before they were finally accepted.

Policy development

During the 1920s, the British government reverted to prewar laissez-faire economic and financial orthodoxy. Spending was reduced in an attempt to balance the budget; an effort was made to repay wartime loans, and monetary policy defended sterling. Persistent unemployment and balance of payments deficits were initially blamed on the war, which had disrupted export markets and increased production costs. The Treasury therefore assumed that restoring economic "normality" required wage reductions to return prices to their prewar levels. This provoked fierce resistance from the unions, stoking fear of socialism – especially when the Treasury unwisely restored the gold standard, revaluing sterling at its prewar 1914 parity. The resulting price deflation squeezed British manufacturers, who tried to limit their losses by cutting wages – precipitating the 1926 General Strike.

However, despite economic, social, and political unrest, high unemployment, and a persistent balance of payments deficit, the Treasury continued to pursue its restrictive economic policy. But the national debt remained largely unaffected.

In 1924, Keynes published an article in *The Times*, "Does Unemployment Need a Drastic Remedy?," arguing that addressing unemployment meant not only monetary reform, but also "the diversion of national savings from relatively barren foreign investment into state-encouraged constructive enterprises at home." Later, in "How to Organize a Wave of Prosperity," he again argued for public spending to combat unemployment; and in 1929, with Hubert Henderson, he wrote the pamphlet, *Can Lloyd George Do It?*, in support of Lloyd George's campaign pledge to reduce unemployment through major public works, financed by borrowing.

However, the British Treasury rejected this idea in its 1929 White Paper, *Memoranda on Certain Proposals Relating to Unemployment*; and in his 1929 budget speech, Winston Churchill reiterated the orthodox Treasury view: "[W]hen the Government borrow[s] in the money market it becomes a new competitor with industry and engrosses to itself resources which would otherwise have been employed by private enterprise, and in the process it raises the rent of money to all who have need of it."

Keynes had often been accused of ignoring the need to maintain confidence in both Britain's financial policies and the country's position in the international community, but he was opposed to fiscal profligacy. In his analysis, austerity was clearly necessary, but only during a boom, when economic growth would support deficit and debt reduction, providing the resources to counter the next recession or avert inflation.

Meanwhile, unemployment continued to climb; and the editor of *The Times* sought economists' opinions about the question of inadequate private spending. Keynes and colleagues at the University of Cambridge sparked a public debate about the economics of government stimulus and austerity by stressing the importance of *both* private *and* public spending to address unemployment caused by low effective demand. Their idea was to mobilize unused, especially human, resources, which would expand aggregate demand. This would mobilize further resources, resulting in a virtuous cycle with multiplier effects, since the total increase in economic activity would be far greater than the government spending that triggered it.

However, the alternative (neoclassical) view had equally vocal proponents in *The Times* debate. Friedrich von Hayek and some of his colleagues at the London School of Economics (LSE) were "of the opinion that many of the troubles of the world at the present time are due to imprudent borrowing and spending on the part of public authorities."[3] They argued that any public spending should involve investment in private businesses, and they set out their case for fiscal austerity and the freeing-up of markets.

Having blamed differing causes for the crisis – insufficient effective demand on the one hand, and insufficient funds for private investment on the other – the opposing factions recommended contrasting policy solutions. The Cambridge economists argued for government borrowing for public works to close the gap between actual and potential demand, while the LSE economists argued for austerity to make space for private investors in the financial markets.

In his 1933 *Means to Prosperity*, Keynes continued to call for fiscal stimulus; and in 1935, Lloyd George again proposed government borrowing for public works to tackle persistent unemployment. Although ministers now felt they ought to be seen to be doing something – and even the Treasury had finally relented – economic recovery was already well under way. However, this wasn't caused by fiscal policy but by *monetary* policy designed for an entirely different purpose. Speculation had forced sterling off the gold standard, with the resulting depreciation causing interest rates to drop. This reduced the cost of servicing the 1917 war loan and triggered a building boom, which led the economy out of recession.

But not everything was rosy; unemployment remained high in the north and the west. Keynes recognized this, as well as the need to prevent other parts of the economy from overheating. So in 1937 he wrote a series of articles in *The Times* on "How to Avoid a Slump." In "The Problem of the Steady Level," he urged that any new productive capacity be located in distressed regions; in "The Right Time for Austerity," he argued that austerity's time had arrived. Since the economy was expanding (as a consequence of rearmament), deflationary policy was now appropriate to avoid inflation and the risk of financial crisis, which would, in turn, precipitate the next slump.

Keynes' alternative strategy would ultimately be enshrined in economic policy during the 1950s and 1960s. However, it was not so much the strength of his arguments that shifted economic thinking and policy; it was the recovery caused by the massive stimulus from World War II that seemed to validate his ideas about the state's role in the economy – and the appropriate context for austerity.

Policy assessment

In any assessment of British interwar policy, it is important to remember that those making the decisions were dealing with an economy experiencing entirely new dynamics. Recessions now came with a much higher price tag for the state – along with lower tax revenues; and while this was reversed during the boom, these were few and far between in interwar Britain.

One effect of the first full set of "automatic stabilizers" was that cutting government spending no longer necessarily resulted in a lower deficit or debt. This rather disconcerting state of affairs caused some to simply assume that the state was still spending too much, resulting in calls for yet more cuts – making the problem even worse. Keynes was among the first to recognize that the economy now worked very differently; so his ideas were addressing an entirely different situation to that faced by earlier generations of political economists.

However, the idea of stimulating the economy during a recession, to get the unemployed off welfare and paying taxes again – and then paying-off the resulting public debt with the increased income generated during the boom – was hard for many to grasp. Countercyclical intervention seemed counter-intuitive. This is largely why so little changed in Britain between

1920 and 1937. It would take the economic boost to demand of another world war to finally settle the debate.

Austerity in Weimar Germany

Following World War I, the Treaty of Versailles imposed war reparations totaling 132 billion gold marks – 260 percent of Germany's 1913 GDP – a demand that was difficult, if not impossible, to meet. Keynes famously denounced these terms and in 1919 resigned from the negotiations. In his view, the reparation bill, and wider inter-allied war debts, had the potential to cause financial collapse and social instability, with serious economic and political repercussions for Europe and the world.

Germany did indeed struggle to pay the reparations. Having lost its prewar industrial export markets and colonies, the country now relied on foreign loans (particularly from the United States). Not only was output severely depressed and unemployment high, but the currency depreciated, while inflation climbed rapidly. To cover its expenditure and service its debts, the government continued to print money, fueling hyperinflation.

From August 1921, Germany bought the foreign currency required for reparation payments at any price, increasing the speed at which the Papiermark (PM) collapsed in international markets. During the first half of 1922, it was valued at 320 marks per US dollar; but by the fall, it was practically worthless. Germany was therefore required to make payments in goods, with French and Belgian troops occupying the main industrial region, to ensure these were made. However, the German government printed yet more money to support a workers' strike, reigniting inflation; and by November 1923, one US dollar cost 4.2 trillion German PM.

Policy aims

Germany's situation was not an enviable one. With war debt and reparations amounting to more than twice Britain's war debt – and a heavily damaged economy – it was hard to see how these obligations, let alone the cost of running the country, could be met. While initial attempts to make the reparation payments might appear to have little to do with austerity, the experience of hyperinflation would have significant implications later on. The first priorities were to curb inflation and restore confidence in the currency.

Policy development

Responding to Germany's currency crisis, and attempting to restore investor confidence and attract foreign capital, Germany introduced a new currency backed by gold, the Rentenmark (RM). In 1924, the RM was itself replaced by the Reichsmark at the ratio of one-to-one; and until the Great Depression it was a very stable currency, encouraging massive foreign capital inflows that dwarfed reparation payments, sparking economic expansion in both the private and public sectors.

The 1920s also brought an expansion of the welfare state. In 1919, a 48-hour workweek and significant improvements in working conditions were introduced. Health insurance was extended, and a series of tax reforms included higher taxes on capital and income tax for the better-off. A right to education for all children followed, while health insurance coverage was extended. Various improvements were made to unemployment benefits, and laws were passed to regulate rents and increase protection for tenants. Between 1924 and 1931, a housing program was also undertaken, with more than two million new homes being constructed and a further 195,000 modernized. All of these, though, would become targets for austerity.

However, the strength of the 1920s expansion, in combination with the memory of earlier hyperinflation, led to wage and salary increases that outpaced productivity gains. As a consequence, German competitiveness was significantly weakened, and in 1928, there was a sharp drop in investment. After the 1929 Wall Street crash, the situation became critical, as capital inflows and the supply of loans to German banks dried up. At the same time, protective trade measures contributed to a sharp decline in Germany's exports, which fed high and rising unemployment.

By 1930, the situation was serious enough for President Hindenburg to dismiss the government and appoint a presidential cabinet under the chancellorship of Heinrich Brüning – with Article 48 of the Weimar Constitution authorizing him to rule through emergency decrees. A central objective was to lower reparation payments, which by 1930 accounted for approximately 20 percent of public spending, which itself represented 29.6 percent of Germany's GDP. In this context, given his commitment to the gold standard, Brüning saw no alternative to harsh austerity measures.

This was popular with employers, since it promised to reduce labor costs, allowing them to lower their prices in world markets, which in turn would boost the national economy. Many felt that the economic crisis was the result of a bloated welfare state, the abuse of social benefits, excessive wages, and short working hours. However, the promised recovery never materialized, since all industrial economies were pursuing similar export strategies, effectively preserving the status quo.

Between 1930 and 1932, Brüning issued four austerity decrees. The *First Emergency Fiscal and Economic Decree* (July 1930) included a reduction in civil service salaries, cuts in state and municipality revenues, a surcharge on income taxes of those earning more than 8,000 Reichsmarks, and restrictions on the regions' share of turnover taxes. This plan was so unpopular in the Reichstag that President Hindenburg dissolved it, and called for new elections. Brüning was returned to government, but the National Socialist German Workers Party (NSDAP) – the Nazis – campaigning on an anti-austerity platform, emerged as the second largest party, increasing its share of the vote by 15.8 percent.

But this electoral verdict against austerity went unheeded, and Brüning continued his program of austerity. The *Second Emergency Fiscal and Economic Decree* (June 1931) brought a new "crisis tax," levying a surcharge on income tax. Brüning officially denounced the war reparations on the grounds that "the limits of what the German people can tolerate have been reached." Although this was quickly followed by official denials that Germany would suspend payments on both reparations and private debts, market confidence had been shaken and Germany struggled even harder to raise capital. Inflows fell sharply and attempts to attract new international loans failed.

The *Third Emergency Fiscal and Economic Decree* (October 1931) eliminated many Reich transfers to the states and municipalities, and restricted the authority of their parliaments. Civil service salaries were reduced again; nearly everyone under 21 was excluded from welfare benefits; unemployment insurance contributions were increased and restrictions were placed on the period of eligibility for payments. The *Fourth* (and final) *Emergency Fiscal and Economic Decree* (December 1931) brought a further cut in civil service salaries, a significant increase in the turnover tax and a general deflation – with simultaneous cuts in interest rates, wages, and prices.

Although Germany was not the only country to experience the economic fallout of the Great Depression, it was the only major industrialized country to implement deep and prolonged austerity measures. Between 1930 and 1932, total nominal public spending was cut by around 30 percent, while total real government expenditure fell by around 15 percent – with the largest cuts being in housing and healthcare. At the same time, total real revenue and real GDP both fell by 15 percent.

Between 1928 and 1932, as a result of the Wall Street crash and Great Depression, global industrial production fell by almost a third. Germany's industry however, was harder hit, with exports falling by 50 percent. Being heavily reliant on foreign loans, which collapsed when lenders withdrew credit, many businesses were forced into insolvency, which, combined with austerity, resulted in an increase in the unemployment rate from 4.3 to 17.4 percent. Large sections of the population were thrown into poverty, and hunger was widespread, with Brüning being dubbed "the hunger chancellor." From peak to trough, Germany's GDP fell by a third.

Meanwhile, while Brüning had been implementing austerity, the Nazis continued their anti-austerity campaign. Twelve days after the fourth emergency decree, Adolf Hitler issued an *Open Letter from Adolf Hitler to the Reich Chancellor – The Great Illusion of the Last Emergency Decree*. In it, he declared that "although that was not the intention, this emergency decree will help my party to victory, and therefore put an end to the illusions of the present System." In May 1932, the Nazis published another pamphlet – *Emergency Economic Program of the NSDAP* – offering "fundamental improvements in agriculture in general, multiple years of taxation exemption for the settlers, cheap loans and the creation of markets by improving transportation routes, and making them less expensive." Promises for highway construction were also effective in boosting popular support, by signaling "economic 'competence' and an end to austerity." The Nazis also promised "to maintain social insurance, which has been driven to collapse by the present System."

On May 30, 1932, Brüning was removed from the Chancellorship and Hindenburg appointed a minority cabinet headed by Franz von Papen, an Independent. On taking office, he introduced a stimulus package, including employment programs, tax credits and subsidies for new employment, public works projects, and agricultural improvement.

By December 1932, the economy was recovering – with GDP growth of 5.8 percent (compared with declines of 7.9 percent between 1931 and 1932, and 8.1 percent between 1930 and 1931); there was even a 7.6 percent reduction in unemployment. However, von Papen had little support in the Reichstag, and although Hindenburg appointed Kurt von Schleicher of the German National People's party (DNVP) as Chancellor, he was himself replaced as a result of the elections of the following March, which delivered both Hitler and the Nazis to government.

Policy assessment

After World War I, Germany struggled with heavy debt – the terms of which were decided by none-too-friendly foreign powers – and an economy that was hardly in the best shape to respond to these demands. Having stabilized the currency, the apparently recovering German economy rapidly became dependent upon foreign capital inflows. The cause of the breakdown, when it came, was a financial crisis originating in the United States. With foreign loans drying up, Germany was suddenly in the unenviable position of having to either print money or impose significant austerity. Neither was without risk. On the one hand, the memory of hyperinflation was still fresh, while, on the other, much would be asked of a population that had already suffered a great deal.

In the end, austerity was chosen; and, as it often does, it resulted in social and political pushback – in this case, as Keynes had warned, of a particularly extreme nature. What the effect of an earlier stimulus package might have been is difficult to say; but it is worth noting that, in the end, very little of the reparations were ever paid.

The American "New Deal" – and "Roosevelt Recession"

Franklin Delano Roosevelt began his first term of office in March 1933 when America was in the depths of the Great Depression, just four years after the peak of prosperity in 1929 – and the Wall Street crash in October that same year.

Between 1931 and 1932, President Herbert Hoover had actively pursued a policy of reflation, by means of public works and financial assistance to agriculture, banking, and industry, that doubled the rate of federal government investment. However, this had little expansionary effect, because this investment was entirely negated by an even larger contraction in public works at the state, county, and city levels. The depression was made still worse during the spring of 1933, when the economy was rocked by a second banking and financial crisis.

Policy aims

The primary objective of Roosevelt's "New Deal" was the relief of poverty and unemployment as well as both agricultural and urban indebtedness. Most of the New Deal measures were enacted rapidly, as a response to the all too obvious urgency of the situation. The emphasis was therefore not only macroeconomic recovery, but also improvements in living standards, working conditions, and social services. These policy aims were effectively two sides of the same coin, as success in one would very likely bring a significant improvement in the other.

Policy development

The main relief program of the New Deal came in the form of the Federal Emergency Relief Act of May 1933, which authorized the federal government to make direct grants to states and other local authorities, which would then be paid out to farmers and the unemployed, to relieve poverty. Legislation authorizing large-scale public works followed shortly afterward. Thus, government spending took two forms: distribution of money directly to consumers through relief programs, and government investment in public works to provide increased employment.

The fact that this extra government spending involved budget deficits and rising national debt soon put it at odds with the traditional principles of "sound" public finance, which required balanced budgets year-on-year. But Roosevelt was cautious and, although the resulting budget deficits were considerable, averaging $3.4 billion per year between 1934 and 1937, they still only amounted to around 4 percent of GDP.

The decision turned out to be the right one: as a result of the New Deal's expansionary measures, the following four years – 1933 through the fall of 1937 – saw a substantial recovery. Annual real GDP growth averaged over 9 percent; unemployment fell from 25 percent in 1933 to 14 percent; and, by the spring of 1937, production, profits, and wages had returned to their pre-crash levels.

This helped Roosevelt win the 1936 presidential election by a landslide, as he took credit for the economic and social gains achieved during his first term of office:

To balance our budget in 1933 or 1934 or 1935 would have been a crime against the American people ... When Americans suffered, we refused to pass by on the other side. Humanity came first ... No one lightly lays a burden on the income of a Nation. But this vicious tightening circle of our declining national income simply had to be broken ... We accepted the final responsibility of Government, after all else had failed, to spend money when no one else had money left to spend.[4]

However, the second Roosevelt administration would bring an experiment with austerity – and along with it, the "Roosevelt Recession," a devastating dip in the Great Depression that lasted from the autumn of 1937 through most of the following year.

Toward the end of 1936, prices had begun to rise more rapidly. This was partly due to external factors, such as the sudden stimulus to American raw materials exports from European rearmament programs and the drought of 1936, which drove-up agricultural commodity prices. However, inflation was also fueled by a sudden increase in consumer demand, caused not by the New Deal as such, but because in 1936 Congress overrode Roosevelt's veto of a large bonus paid to the veterans of World War I. The following spring, price increases brought commodity speculation and a large rise in business inventories.

The inflationary effects of these developments alarmed the Roosevelt administration; opponents of the New Deal – especially big business and finance – became increasingly vocal about the threat of excessive inflation. They also claimed that the New Deal had harmed business expansion as a result of its threat of both anti-trust legal attacks on large corporations and support for strike action by the American Federation of Labor and Congress of Industrial Organizations (AFL-CIO), as a consequence of the 1935 National Labor Relations Act, which established the legal right of most workers to organize or join labor unions and to bargain collectively with their employers.

Believing that the economy had now acquired sufficient momentum to encourage the private sector to take over leading the recovery, in early 1937, on the advice of his Treasury Secretary Henry Morgenthau, Roosevelt gave in to both his own concerns and those of big business, taking vigorous steps to fight inflation aa well as fiscal deficits. This involved reversing much of the New Deal, with federal government expenditure being curtailed by 17 percent; meanwhile, on top of the tax increases mandated by the Revenue Act of 1935, the 1937 Social Security payroll tax was imposed.

Monetary policy was similarly contractionary. During the spring of 1937, the Federal Reserve (Fed) raised reserve ratios twice in an effort to limit expansion of bank credit; but banks, still nervous after the financial panic of the early 1930s, responded by reducing lending, adding further to the dampening effect of the Fed's policy. This was made still worse by the Treasury's decision to sterilize gold inflows, to reduce excessive reserves, and halt what had been a strong monetary expansion.

These austerity measures did indeed succeed in checking the symptoms of inflation – but at the cost of bringing the American economic recovery to an abrupt halt. The result was a disastrous slump that threatened to eliminate the New Deal's hard-won gains. According to the National Bureau of Economic Research (NBER), the contraction was America's third worst recession of the twentieth century.

Profits fell sharply. The inventory boom and stock market collapsed, with the Dow Jones industrial average dropping 48 percent from its peak in 1937. This, in turn, wiped out the wealth effect of rising stock prices, undermined confidence, and brought back painful memories of the financial crashes of 1929 and 1933. Real GDP fell by 10 percent and national income by 13 percent. Industrial production dropped by 32 percent, with durable goods production falling even faster. Unemployment, which had declined considerably after 1933, rose to 20 percent, with around 4.5 million workers losing their jobs. Falling prices swiftly led to deflation, with wages falling 35 percent.

Realizing that the economy was again heading for a prolonged depression – and ignoring the advice of Treasury – the Roosevelt administration abandoned efforts to balance the budget, calling for the immediate resumption of large-scale government spending on relief and public works, which Congress duly authorized in July 1937. Simply announcing these measures caused an immediate stock market recovery; and from July onward, economic recovery proceeded apace.

However, although the American economy began to recover in mid-1938, employment did not regain its early 1937 level until the United States entered World War II in late 1941. After this, productivity steadily increased, with output and employment in 1942 reaching levels well above those of 1929 and 1937.

Policy assessment

Perhaps the most interesting part of Roosevelt's New Deal is that much of it was aimed at alleviating the suffering of the American people, rather than focusing only on measures of macroeconomic performance. This is not to say that these measures didn't drive macroeconomic recovery – they certainly did, although that was not necessarily the primary concern. The American approach stands in stark contrast to that of both Britain and Germany between the wars, whose focus was on "sound" public finance. In both, the result was considerable social suffering and unrest, leading to political change. By contrast, Roosevelt was easily re-elected. Nor did the travails endured by Britain and Germany prove worth the investment in financial terms, with macroeconomic measures of success remaining stubbornly unaffected.

But perhaps the most eye-catching aspect of the New Deal was the speed of the recovery. In both 1933 and 1938, the economic response was almost immediate, with even the announcement of renewed federal spending in 1938 being enough to mitigate the Roosevelt Recession. This effectively highlights a lack of confidence in the private sector that is usually associated with a recession – and why it is usually the state that needs to rebuild some of that confidence if a recovery is to be encouraged.

Also noteworthy is the speed with which the financial sector – in this case including the Fed – can rapidly, and dramatically, affect the real economy. While the financial sector's part in the Wall Street crash is well known, its contribution to the slump of 1937–8, following the withdrawal of credit, has a much lower profile. Again, the speed of the impact stands out. While the excessive credit of the "Roaring Twenties" took nearly a decade to result in trouble, the effect of a lack of credit in 1937–8 was immediate.

These can be compared with the effects of stimulus and austerity. An economy cannot be stimulated permanently without at some point overheating; but it will usually take time to get there. The effect of austerity on an economy, however, is typically immediate. As this case shows, the dampening effect is not limited to finance, where it also undermines confidence. Confidence in the economy as a whole is as important as confidence in the currency.

Perhaps the best assessment of the effectiveness of Roosevelt's policies, though, is that of the American electorate. His response to the worst depression the country had yet seen got him re-elected by a landslide. Not many leaders in Britain or Germany could say the same.

Conclusions

The experiences of both Weimar Germany and Great Britain between the wars clearly demonstrate that the introduction of various kinds of automatic stabilizer had completely changed the game. In Britain, new economic theories incorporating these changed dynamics were advanced – in particular by Keynes – to develop appropriate policies to address them. These prioritized economic growth (rather than austerity) as the best means of reducing public debt. The dynamics at work in these cases also show that, by the early twentieth century, the comparison between a business or household budget and its sovereign counterpart no longer made any sense.

But it was not just the *economic* dynamics that had changed: social and political dynamics had, too. The poor and unemployed, who now relied on welfare spending, were inclined to react badly to any reduction in state support – let alone harsh austerity. Worse still, for established political parties, suffrage was becoming more widespread. So the growing number of poor voters could now influence the government's budget, and if they didn't like any of the choices on offer, they could set up a new political party to push their own agenda. This was the case in Britain as well as in Germany; and in both, these new political movements were influenced by the condition of the working classes – and hence austerity.

In interwar Britain, austerity caused so much social and labor unrest that it stoked fear of a socialist revolution; it also caused a split within the Liberal Party and a strengthening of the nascent Labour Party. In the end, social breakdown was avoided – probably because of the protection provided for the most vulnerable groups in society by the Liberal Party's prewar social reforms – as well as the timing of austerity. When the Great Depression arrived, the worst of Britain's own depression had passed, with the 1931 sterling devaluation not only reducing the cost of financing the war loan, but also triggering a building boom in much of England. By the early 1930s, the Treasury had also finally given up its resistance to stimulus.

By contrast, in Weimar Germany, having responded successfully to the crisis caused by the hyperinflation of the early 1920s, foreign capital flowed into Germany's financial markets, powering economic expansion and wide-ranging social reforms. However, the Wall Street Crash abruptly cut off the flow of investment from America, causing an immediate economic and political crisis – especially as Germany could no longer make its reparation payments. In this context, Brüning's commitment to the gold standard, plus his feeling that the welfare state was part of the problem, motivated severe and prolonged austerity. Worse still, this was implemented during the Great Depression – which leveraged its negative effects beyond even those of a "normal" recession. The result was soaring unemployment, poverty, and economic hardship for large segments of the population. But despite this, Brüning persisted – even while the Nazis launched an anti-austerity campaign that ultimately brought Hitler to power in 1933. This demonstrates that cutting social welfare during a severe depression could be a very dangerous political gamble indeed.

The effect of "automatic stabilizers" was less obvious in the US, where welfare, in particular, took a rather different – and more limited – form, and where the introduction of an income tax had been slower in gaining ground. Nonetheless, the Russian Revolution was still only a couple of decades in the past, so governments on both sides of the Atlantic were likely to be all too aware of the possible impact of a seriously discontented workforce with very little left to lose.

As a result, the stimulus of the New Deal wasn't so much an automatic response as a considered one, based on targeting the key problem areas. The success of this was soon clear, with only finance and large corporations feeling that they were not among the winners from the package. As it turned out, both these sectors were abruptly proven wrong, by the disastrous economic results of Roosevelt giving in to a combination of their demands and his own nervousness over inflation.

It is also worth noting that countercyclical policy was hardly unknown in the US, with a strong cadre of economists thinking along very similar lines to Keynes in Britain. However, while the Americans were comfortable with the idea that stimulus was an effective response to recession, Keynes's own compatriots were far slower to unlearn their traditional ideas, with the result that both they – and the unhelpful effects of their policies – would persist in Britain.

Overall, the British, German, and American experiences between the wars demonstrate that austerity during a recession will not only produce negative economic effects, but, very probably, radical social and political ones as well. They also show that reducing state spending during a slump will leverage the automatic stabilizers and raise the fiscal multiplier, defeating the aims of austerity by increasing both the government's deficit and its debt – and further shrinking an already contracting economy.

6

Austerity (and Stimulus) in Postwar Chile, America, Ireland, and Japan

Introduction

This chapter looks at some of the more extreme cases involving austerity, offering something of a verdict on a number of the more technical arguments used to support them. Once again, the part played by timing will be clear.

Chile offers an insight into the effects of unrestricted austerity, which was allowed to run its full course under a military dictatorship, unhindered by the usual social and labor resistance. But would the economic outcomes match predictions? "Reaganomics" offers an example of the ideology of austerity driving efforts to reduce the economic and social welfare role of the state. Although these efforts were effective in linking welfare to work, whether they shrunk the size and influence of the American state is open to debate. The Irish case puts the concept of "expansionary austerity" to the test. As the most frequently quoted example of this concept, the results should be clear; but did austerity drive GDP growth – or did growth make room for austerity? Finally, economic policy in Japan offers a contrasting view to Reinhardt and Rogoff's opinion that public debt-to-GDP ratios in excess of 90 percent cause GDP growth to contract – so what happens when the public debt-to-GDP ratio approaches three times that level?

Austerity in Pinochet's Chile

On September 11, 1973, the government of Salvador Allende – the first democratically elected Marxist president of a Latin American country – was overthrown by a military coup d'état, led by General Augusto Pinochet. Before this, Chile had been considered a politically stable constitutional democracy; and three years earlier, Allende had promised a "Chilean road to socialism" based on democratic principles. The new government quickly launched reforms, all within the national constitution. Keynesian measures were used to increase wages and salaries, stimulating demand and producing a "consumer revolution" (since prices were held down). Copper mines (both domestic- and foreign-owned) were nationalized, along with oligopolistic industries and banks. Most large agricultural estates were taken into state ownership, the land being returned to resident workers, and many factories were turned over to collective management by workers and the state.

All this deeply antagonized Chile's business community – especially its American multinationals – while the middle and upper classes worried about popular revolution. Given the ongoing Cold War, there were also concerns about socialism – or, worse, communism – spreading to more of Latin America. On June 27, 1970, Henry Kissinger, US President Nixon's Security Advisor, reportedly told the Forty Committee, a secret operations group he directed: "I don't see why we need to stand by and watch a country go Communist due to the irresponsibility of its own people."[1] So, with the support of the US government, the Central Intelligence Agency (CIA), and multinational businesses, even before Allende came to power, Chile's business clans planned to topple him.

Policy aims

In some ways, austerity represents a direction of travel. As well as withdrawing public support and services, it also minimizes the role of the state as an economic actor. In this case, the main objectives were clear: first, the removal of a Marxist economy, close to the US homeland during the Cold War, and, second, preservation of the interests of American multinationals. To what extent the economic theories developed at the University of Chicago were, at that point, intended to influence subsequent developments is not entirely clear. But "the Brick" – an economic action plan prepared in advance by the "Chicago Boys" for just such an event as Pinochet's coup – strongly suggests that they were on the agenda.

Policy development

Following the coup, Pinochet swiftly reversed Allende's reforms, returning nationalized enterprises to their former owners, compensating multinational companies affected by expropriation measures, liberalizing markets, eliminating price controls, and freeing up interest rates. There was also an unsuccessful attempt to stabilize the macroeconomy; but inflation remained persistently high, in the range of 400 to 500 percent, discouraging foreign direct investment (FDI). Meanwhile, a sharp fall in copper prices – Chile's principal export – widened the trade deficit. The spike in oil prices following the 1973 OPEC oil shock depressed manufacturing even further. By 1975, the economy was deep in recession.

In response, Pinochet, without an economic plan of his own, handed the problem over to a group of economists known as the "Chicago boys," suppressing any opposition to their policies. The Chicago boys had all studied at the University of Chicago between 1955 and 1963, under Milton Friedman; by the end of 1974, they were all in positions of power, controlling most of Chile's economic planning offices.

In March 1975, the Chicago boys organized a conference, inviting some of the world's top economists, including Milton Friedman and Arnold Harberger. With extensive media coverage, a radical austerity program – "shock treatment" – was presented as the solution to Chile's economic problems. It called for a dramatic reduction in both government expenditure and the money supply, the privatization of public services, extensive market deregulation, and international trade liberalization. Adding its support to that of Friedman and Harberger, the

IMF and the World Bank made this program a precondition for any future loans to Chile.

Shortly afterwards, Chile's "Economic Recovery Program" (ERP) was introduced; and following deregulation, oligopolies appeared in almost all sectors of the economy, while the elimination of restrictions on FDI brought a tripling of foreign loans. Deep cuts in public spending and the money supply proved successful in reducing inflation – but only at the expense of output (which fell by 12.9 percent) and unemployment (which more than doubled, to 18.7 percent), producing Chile's worst recession since the Great Depression.[2] To mitigate the political consequences, the regime banned all opposition parties, suspended labor unions, and cracked down on potential opposition leaders.

By mid-1976, the economy began to recover. Inflation fell to below 100 percent, as a result of exchange rate devaluation. Meanwhile, increasing world copper prices and stronger export growth contributed to an improvement in the balance of payments. Between 1978 and 1981, GDP growth expanded at an annual rate of 6.6 percent, which was branded an "Economic Miracle"; and in 1982, Friedman praised Pinochet for his adherence to "a fully free-market economy as a matter of principle."[3]

However, Chilean unemployment still averaged 15.7 percent, the worst in Latin America, with damaging effects on productivity. Also, much of Chile's growth came from unproductive sectors of the economy, including financial services, where speculators had been attracted by the country's interest rates, which, in 1977 were the highest in the world, at 51 percent. Worse still, when both the recession and recovery were taken into account, between 1975 and 1980, Chile's rate of growth was the second worst in Latin America, higher only than that of Argentina.[4]

In September 1979, Pinochet announced that economic restructuring was complete and the government would now focus on "national modernization."[5] The "Seven Modernizations" extended marketization to labor, social security, education, agriculture, and the justice system; it also included administrative and regionalization reforms. Labor reform greatly reduced trade union power, placing severe limitations on the right to strike and fragmenting the labor movement.

The pay-as-you-go social security system was turned into an individual savers' scheme, where mandatory contributions were paid to private institutions, which invested them in the stock market. "Modernization" in other social sectors also sought to develop markets, with the government guaranteeing minimum free services for only the very poor.

In 1980, the Pinochet government, having consulted Friedrich von Hayek personally, adopted a new political constitution and named it after Hayek's book, *The Constitution of Liberty*. It placed strong emphasis on a definition of freedom based on private property, freedom of enterprise, and individual rights; and it committed the government to guaranteeing a free market order. Stressing the necessity of a strong central authority to protect individual freedom and free market conditions against both "totalitarian attacks" and "democratic intervention," it gave the President unquestioned authority, but limited the state's discretionary power to establishing the rule of law and suppressing opposition. The new constitution established a transition period of seventeen years before presidents would be democratically elected. For the first eight, Parliament and political parties were banned; and in the ninth, the constitution would be fully applicable, following a referendum on Pinochet's continued rule.

However, an economic crisis in 1982 slowed the reform process. Integration into world markets had exposed Chile to international market forces and it was hit harder than any other Latin American country by the global recession. World copper prices fell sharply; foreign capital markets dried up, and the interest on Chile's massive debt – mostly incurred through consumption, mergers and acquisitions, and speculative investments – sky-rocketed. By 1983, the economy was in crisis; manufacturing output fell 28 percent, while unemployment rose to 34.6 percent.[6] To avert financial collapse, the government rescued Chile's largest financial groups, transferring their debts to the government balance sheet at a cost of 3 percent of GDP for each of the next three years, which was passed on to taxpayers. Loans were offered by the IMF – but came with yet more austerity conditions.

By 1984, the Chilean economy had again begun to recover; and between 1986 and 1989, average annual GDP growth was around 7 percent. However, 1989 per capita GDP was still 6.1 percent *below* its 1981 level. Considering the Pinochet era as a whole (1973–89), per capita GDP actually *fell* by 6.4 percent, total GDP increased more slowly than it had during the 1960s, and Chile's economic performance ranked among the bottom six Latin American countries.[7]

Social and living standards also deteriorated. Encouraged by the IMF and the World Bank, high unemployment was a deliberate part of austerity policy, driving down wages, as unemployed workers competed for the few jobs available, accepting sub-poverty wages to get them. Between 1970 and 1989, labor's share of national income fell from 52.3 to 30.7 percent, with the poverty rate reaching 41.2 percent in 1989, one-third of which included the "indigent or desperately poor."[8] Meanwhile, the proportion of Chileans without adequate housing increased from 27 percent to 40 percent between 1972 and 1988. However, the richest 10 percent of Chileans saw their share of national income increase from 36.5 percent to 46.8 percent between 1980 and 1989, whilst the share received by the bottom half of income earners decreased, from 20.4 percent to 16.8 percent.[9]

In 1988, the government honored its constitutional commitment to a referendum on Pinochet's presidency for another eight years. Pinochet lost the vote and in 1989 was replaced by Patricio Aylwin, a moderate Christian Democrat. Pinochet remained as head of the military until 1998.

The legacy of this experiment with extreme economic austerity continues to the present. Although making a peaceful transition to democracy in 1990, Chile's economic performance still lags behind most other Latin American countries. Much of its industry is foreign-owned, so profits do not stay in the country; it continues to have one of the largest foreign debt levels in the world; and inequality and poverty remain high.

Policy assessment

In terms of removing a Marxist economy in close proximity to the United States – and supporting the American multinational businesses operating there – the Pinochet government's experiment with austerity was clearly successful. However, it is doubtful whether a policy package like that which followed the coup would have been possible or sustainable without the military dictatorship. As Europe is being reminded at the time of writing, sustained extreme austerity often has socially and politically destabilizing results; and these can serve as a catalyst for the rise of popular opposition movements.

Setting aside the social and political dimensions, however, perhaps the main question is the degree to which Pinochet's austerity could be considered an *economic* success. In this, it is very difficult to regard any of the outcomes as delivering against the promise of economic prosperity – in absolute or comparative terms. Per capita GDP deteriorated significantly, growth in total GDP slowed, national debt levels remained high, and Chile's economic performance relative to its Latin American neighbors was dismal.

Ronald Reagan's "Selective Austerity"

The American welfare state had developed in two main stages, largely in response to social crises. As we saw in Chapter 5, the New Deal was a pragmatic response to the Great Depression. The second major expansion accompanied the Johnson administration's "Great Society" programs, aimed at eliminating the roots and symptoms of urban poverty, which had become apparent during the 1960s; and between 1960 and 1975, social welfare expenditure significantly increased.

The "stagflationary" crises of the 1970s, however, called the viability of this state of affairs into question; and economic thinking shifted toward the pre-Keynesian idea that poverty and unemployment were the result of choices made by those afflicted, rather than being systemic problems, resulting from insufficient effective demand. It also undermined confidence in the government's role in managing the economy. In Ronald Reagan's 1981 inaugural address, after describing the "economic affliction of great proportions" confronting his administration, he famously declared: "In this present crisis, government is not the solution to the problem; government is the problem."[10]

Policy aims

Reagan had been elected by a landslide and came to the White House promising smaller government, reduced taxes, and lower inflation – capitalizing on public fear and confusion about uncontrolled inflation and unemployment. However, during the 1980s, austerity would be selectively applied to social welfare expenditure. The ultimate aim was to significantly reduce the size and importance of the welfare state, with Reagan's long-term objective being the federal government's withdrawal from social welfare provision altogether.

Policy development

Within seven months of Reagan's inauguration, Congress enacted the largest cuts in taxes and social welfare in American history. The 1981 Economic Recovery Tax Act (ERTA) lowered marginal income tax rates, with the top rate falling from 70 to 50 percent (and then to 28 percent), and the bottom rate from 14 to 11 percent; it also significantly reduced estate and corporation taxes. "Supply-side" economics provided the rationale for these deep cuts, the idea being that they would more than pay for themselves through a boost to economic growth, caused by increased incentives to save, invest, and work. This, it was hoped, would generate *increased* tax revenues and balance the budget.

The spending cuts were introduced quickly through "budget reconciliation," a process established by the 1974 Congressional Budget Reconciliation Act, designed to help Congress bring government spending and revenue in line with the priorities set out in the annual budget resolution, with the aim of slowing spending growth and reducing the deficit. The Omnibus Budget Reconciliation Act of 1981 (OBRA) lowered and narrowed the US social safety net by restricting eligibility criteria, reducing benefits, and clamping down on users of multiple programs, with means-tested programs being hardest hit. The act also devolved responsibility for welfare to the states. But with a severe recession leading to an increase in the number of poor people, at the same time as OBRA reduced support levels, welfare spending was largely unaffected.

The combined effect of ERTA – which caused a sharp fall (rather than the predicted boost) in tax revenues – and OBRA, was a rising federal deficit and expanding public debt. Worse still, with interest rates above 20 percent, the economy fell into the second dip of the 1978–82 recession, the most serious downturn since the Great Depression, with unemployment reaching a postwar high of 10 percent.

In response, Congress quickly enacted the 1982 Tax Equity and Fiscal Responsibility Act (TEFRA), which rolled back (but did not entirely reverse) the ERTA tax cuts. The government also tried to cut the benefits provided by the long-standing Old-Age Survivors Insurance program, better known as "Social Security." This, however, was met with such strong resistance that the Republican-controlled Senate was ultimately forced to vote against the president. By 1982, though, projections that the Social Security Trust Fund would run out of money the following year motivated the establishment of the National Commission on Social Security Reform, chaired by Alan Greenspan. The Social Security Amendments of 1983 – which amounted to the second largest tax increase of the 1980s (after TEFRA) – raised social security payroll tax rates, reduced benefits, and lowered retirement rates.

By 1983, inflation had also been reduced (but only after the economy was plunged into recession), and the economy was in recovery, brought about by massive federal deficits, rising military expenditure, and reductions in interest rates engineered by the Fed. However, the cuts in social welfare were generating increasing poverty and inequality, while homelessness was becoming an increasingly visible problem. Between 1980 and 1984, the Gini coefficient (where 0 represents complete equality and 1 complete inequality) rose from 0.379 to 0.401, and the proportion of households receiving less than 50 percent of the median income increased from 15.9 percent to 18.2 percent. At the same time, the income share of the top 1 percent of households grew from 8.18 percent to 8.89 percent. and the earnings of the top 10 percent of households as a percentage of the median climbed from 194 percent to 207 percent.[11]

The attitude of the Reagan administration toward the poor, however, was dismissive. In an interview with the *Wall Street Journal*, Reagan observed that "if there are individuals who suffer from our economic program, they are people who have been dropped from various things like food stamps because they weren't morally eligible for them ... in many cases, weren't even technically eligible for them."[12]

Nevertheless, during the 1984 presidential election, "fairness" was a significant issue – as were public deficits (which averaged 4.01 percent between 1981 and 1984) and debt (which rose from 40.33 percent to 49.51 percent of GDP).[13] With these opposing priorities, financial concerns won out, and Reagan easily gained a second term in office.

Political pressure on spending, resulting from large budget deficits, led to the 1985 Balanced Budget and Emergency Control Act, which set a deficit ceiling on each fiscal year, reaching zero by 1991. Were the budget balance to exceed these limits, automatic cuts, falling equally on defense and non-defense spending would bring it back within the limits. However, the Act failed to rein in the deficits.

In Reagan's 1986 State of the Union Address, social welfare reform linking welfare to work entered the national agenda:

> After hundreds of billions of dollars in poverty programs, the plight of the poor grows more painful. But the waste in dollars and cents pales before the most tragic loss: the sinful waste of human spirit and potential. We can ignore this terrible truth no longer. As Franklin Roosevelt warned 51 years ago, standing before this Chamber, he said, "Welfare is a narcotic, a subtle destroyer of the human spirit." And we must now escape the spider's web of dependency.

Reagan then announced that he would direct the White House Domestic Policy Council to re-evaluate the entire US welfare system.

The 1987 Family Security, Family Welfare, and Welfare Independence Acts all linked welfare reform to work. But it was the 1988 Family Support Act (FSA) that cemented this link by forcing paid work on welfare recipients, with little regard for the adequacy of pay – and adding to the already growing numbers of working poor. The FSA also consolidated and extended many of the 1981 welfare reforms and gave states greater control over its provision.

However, public spending continued to increase, largely as a result of military expenditure, which rose to around 6 percent of GDP, the highest rate since the end of the Vietnam War in 1973. When Reagan left office, aside from inflation, almost all the major macroeconomic indicators had deteriorated.

Manufacturing had lost a million jobs, public debt was 60.15 percent of GDP, and the US was now the largest international debtor, having previously been the largest creditor nation. Poverty and inequality increased even further, with the Gini coefficient reaching 0.414, while the income share of the top 1 percent of households rose by 13.17 percent and the earnings of the top 10 percent of households as a percent of the median reached 210 percent of the median.

Policy assessment

Overall, Reagan's "selective" austerity can be seen as an example of ideologically driven austerity. Spending cuts were largely aimed at the welfare state and those dependent on it. The program of austerity was – officially, at least – triggered by the usual concerns about public deficits and debt. But there was no clear attempt to address them through austerity, especially given the sharp rise in military spending and the extensive program of tax cuts – the budget reductions were all squarely aimed at welfare provision.

Judging success against his stated aims for austerity, Reagan's administration did not have much to celebrate. Public deficits remained high and debt rapidly increased; and while welfare as a proportion of total federal spending did indeed fall faster than during the 1970s, this was as much the result of greatly increased military spending plus higher interest payments on the national debt as it was reduced welfare spending.

Federal welfare spending as a proportion of GDP also declined; but this, too, was in no small part due to other factors – in this case, the devolution of responsibility for welfare to the states, causing a corresponding increase in state and local welfare spending. Meanwhile, federal spending on some programs – such as Social Security and Medicare – actually increased as a result of population aging.

Ireland and "Expansionary Austerity"

By the end of the 1980s, high levels of public debt led to renewed interest in the economics of austerity, including the effect of government deficits and debt on both inflation and balance of payments problems – especially in the run-up to the introduction of the euro. The Maastricht Treaty's "convergence criteria" required EU member states adopting the euro to set strict limits on public deficits and debt, stipulating that annual public deficits could not exceed 3 percent of GDP, while debt-to-GDP ratios must be under 60 percent. To meet these criteria, prospective members would be required to reduce spending on welfare, which would inevitably have social and political consequences. This sparked interest in countries that had apparently managed to grow despite significant austerity, producing the novel idea of "expansionary fiscal consolidation."

The research suggesting that austerity had expansionary effects was soon discredited. However, following the 2008 financial crisis, advocates of austerity resurrected the idea, claiming that it would boost economic performance. The most popular apparent exemplar of "expansionary austerity" was Ireland during the late 1980s, which, it was argued, ultimately gave rise to the "Celtic Tiger" economy.

Policy aims

The 1970s and 1980s were challenging for Ireland. In response, the government embarked on a series of deficit spending policies, resulting in very high levels of public debt, at the same time as rising interest rates made servicing that debt increasingly unaffordable. But due to political concerns, Ireland's debt problem went unaddressed until 1987, when the minority Fianna Fáil government adopted a strategy of economic reform, aimed at reducing fiscal deficits and public debt.

Policy development

During the second half of the 1950s, in response to a deep recession, the Irish government began opening the economy up to foreign competition and shifting from agriculture toward industry. In 1956, tax relief on export profits of both domestic- and foreign-owned businesses was introduced; and a detailed study of the economy was commissioned, which in 1958 produced a White Paper, "The First Programme for Economic Expansion," recommending policies for growth, including investment in industrial infrastructure and tax incentives for export-oriented FDI.

During the 1960s, these policies proved successful and the economy expanded, with annual GDP growth of around 4 percent from 1959 to 1973. The resulting increase in public revenue was invested in social infrastructure; and the government adopted policies to improve productivity, including educational reforms and the promotion of high-tech export-oriented industries. Emigration fell as living standards improved; and by the late 1960s, Ireland's industrial workforce outnumbered those in agriculture, for the first time. From the early 1970s onward, as a consequence of these policies, Irish productivity growth consistently outpaced other advanced economies.

In 1973, Ireland joined the European Economic Community (EEC), initiating a catching-up process with the rest of Europe. However, the 1973 OPEC oil shock plunged the world economy into a stagflationary crisis and recession, which reduced demand for Irish exports, while domestic costs were rising rapidly. In an attempt to maintain employment and living standards, the government implemented a program of deficit spending.

In 1979, Ireland joined the European Monetary System (EMS), which had the effect of overvaluing the currency and undermining export competitiveness. In an attempt to prop up the currency, government borrowing increased, adding to already high levels of debt, which became increasingly costly to service. By 1981, with a fiscal deficit of 11.1 percent of GDP, and a debt-to-GDP ratio approaching 70 percent, the newly elected Prime Minister Charles Haughey declared: "We are living away beyond our means ... we are borrowing enormous sums of money ... at a rate that just cannot continue ... we have got to cut down government spending."[14]

But this wasn't Ireland's only problem. The country was also struggling with high unemployment, industrial unrest, mass emigration, and political instability and corruption – with power alternating between Fianna Fáil and Fine Gael. With the political risks of cutting public spending apparently outweighing the economic benefits, the public debt went unaddressed. By 1987, the debt-to-GDP ratio had reached 108.6

percent, with an annual interest cost of nearly 10 percent of GDP; tax rates were also punitively high, due to failed attempts to stabilize the deficit; and growth was stagnant. At this point, the minority Fianna Fáil government began a process of economic reform, which was largely continued by successive governments. With the aim of reducing public deficits and debt, austerity measures involved capital account spending cuts, current account spending restraint (but not at the expense of social welfare), and reduced borrowing to fund current spending. Reforms also focused on promoting competition, reducing taxes, and combating tax evasion.

At the same time, the EMS stabilized and membership in the European Union (EU) brought both access to EU funding and lower interest rates, making the debt more manageable and aiding expansion. A well-timed devaluation in 1986 contributed to the improved competitiveness of Irish exports, which were boosted by the "Lawson boom" in the UK, Ireland's major trading partner. The macroeconomic expansion in the UK, associated with the policies of Margaret Thatcher's Chancellor of the Exchequer Nigel Lawson, resulted in strong UK demand for Irish exports. FDI was also up, attracted by very low tax rates, by Ireland's productive, well-educated, and English-speaking workforce at relatively low wages, and by access to the European single market. In a series of agreements between the Irish government, unions, and business associations – known as the "social partnership" – gradual pay increases were exchanged for industrial peace, with the average wage rising by over 14 percent between 1986 and 1989, and a comparable increase in public sector pay.

All of this supported expansion of the Irish economy; and, as it turned out, the timing of Irish austerity coincided with a strengthening recovery, with GDP growth – which was already 4.7 percent by 1987 – rising steadily to a peak of 8.5 percent in 1990.[15] By 1989, Ireland's debt was far more sustainable, with the fiscal deficit falling to 2.2 percent of GDP and the public debt-to-GDP ratio dropping below 100 percent. But it wasn't until 1997 that the fiscal balance was in surplus, where it remained until 2007 – aside from a brief recession in 2002, following the collapse of the "dot-com" bubble. With annual GDP growth averaging 6.3 percent between 1987 and 2007 and fiscal surpluses averaging 1.6 percent of GDP between 1997 and 2007, public debt was steadily reduced, standing at 27 percent of GDP in 2007 – just prior to the arrival of the 2008 crisis.

Policy assessment

Given the composition and timing of Ireland's austerity measures, it is difficult to argue that they were the cause of the country's economic expansion. While the policy package clearly included restraint in both current and capital account spending as well as tax increases, spending on social welfare and other key public services was not cut. The timing also worked in Ireland's favor, with austerity being implemented when stabilization of the EMS and access to EU funding and lower interest rates made it far easier to manage public debt; and Ireland's 1986 devaluation – which coincided with the "Lawson boom" – provided a boost for Irish exports.

Since austerity was introduced at a time when the Irish economy was already strengthening sufficiently to withstand it, the evidence suggests that – rather than austerity being expansionary – GDP growth provided the context within which it could operate effectively in reducing public deficits and debt.

Japan: Does a Public Debt-to-GDP Ratio of 90 Percent Really Mark a "Stagnation Threshold"?

Western economies were not the only ones stepping into the unknown during the 1970s, with seemingly intractable economic problems – such as stagflation – apparently being the norm instead of the exception. Japan, one of the more Westernized Asian nations, faced many of the same problems, but addressed them in a generally more collective manner. Austerity – "fiscal reconstruction" in its Japanese guise – played a part in the evolving policy package, but was rarely dominant.

Policy aims

Japanese public policy has generally been geared toward longer-term stability; but this hasn't ruled out experiments with new ideas – including austerity. The Japanese approach to both stimulus and austerity has been overwhelmingly countercyclical. So this case study overviews policy – punctuated by booms, downturns, and the effects of a regional financial crisis – rather than assessing the Japanese response to a single event.

Policy development

Japan is an island nation with a strong collective identity, which has had a significant influence on the development of its social and economic policy, the general aim of which has been to support society. But in an economy with a strong manufacturing base, that means supporting industry as well.

The Japanese government traditionally pursued a balanced budget policy, maintaining fiscal balance until 1965, when the first postwar bonds were issued. But following the oil shock of 1973–4, the deficit expanded rapidly, with an accompanying increase in public debt. This was partly due to the costs of dealing with the resulting recession and new spending on welfare during the first half of the decade, public investment to counter recession during the second – and falling tax revenues during both. Japan now had to decide what attitude to take toward public debt.

Seemingly overnight, falling oil supplies and rising prices powered inflation, while slower growth produced Japan's first industrial downturn since the Korean War. Between 1973 and 1974, GDP growth collapsed, from an annual increase of 8 percent to a contraction of 1.2 percent. However, driven by a surge in exports, the economy recovered rapidly: by 1979, GDP growth was 5.5 percent, well above that of other industrial countries at the time.

Renewed economic growth and progress on deficit reduction were not, however, immune to the effects of a second OPEC oil shock in 1979 and the outbreak of the Iran–Iraq war. GDP growth slowed to 2.8 percent in 1980, with the deficit fluctuating between 4.5 percent and 5.5 percent between

1978 and 1980. As concerns about the macroeconomic effects of growing fiscal deficits increased, the government adopted "fiscal reconstruction" – austerity – aimed at eliminating it. The Ministry of Finance pressured other ministries to hold down expenditure; and in 1982, a ceiling of zero growth in budget requests was imposed, which was later tightened to negative increases.

With the inflation of Japan's "bubble economy" during the second half of the 1980s, sharp increases in stock and real estate prices not only spurred GDP growth; they also increased revenues from corporate security transactions and capital gains taxes. With this extra income, austerity helped reduce accumulated deficits; and by 1988, the fiscal balance was in surplus and the aim of fiscal reconstruction achieved.

The inevitable collapse of Japan's bubble economy was sudden. In 1991, the Nikkei index, having peaked at 39,000 on the last day of trading in 1989, abruptly fell to 14,000, bottoming out at 8,000 (almost 80 percent below its peak) just over a decade later, with real estate prices following a similar trajectory. As the crisis spilled over into the real economy, GDP growth also dropped, from a peak of 7.1 percent in 1988 to 0.2 percent in 1993. Japanese manufacturing, having increased capacity during the boom, now looked for ways of cutting costs, laying-off workers, and moving production to China and Southeast Asia. This resulted in increased unemployment – unheard of in postwar Japan with the official rate rising from 2.1 percent in 1991 to 5.4 percent in 2002, although economists estimated that the *actual* rates were more than double these figures.

Tax revenues fell sharply, intensifying pressure to counter the recession with expansionary policies. In response, the Japanese government announced the first of several stimulus measures, concentrated in August 1992 to September 1995 and April 1998 to October 2000. However, in 1993, the Liberal Democratic Party (LDP), which had vacillated on the question of economic policy, lost power for the first time since 1955, ushering in a period of political instability.

Nevertheless, in both phases of fiscal expansion, the government focused expenditure on public investment – mainly infrastructure – along with real estate purchases and loans to the financial and housing sectors. Initially, it was less aggressive with tax policy. The April 1993 budget brought a negligible tax reduction, with a larger one in the February 1994 stimulus package, when income taxes were reduced by 5.9 trillion yen (about 1.2 percent of GDP), with the expectation that any losses in revenue would be countered by higher value-added taxes (VAT). Lower current taxes and anticipation of higher consumption taxes in the near future shifted consumption forward, providing a brief stimulus and increasing average GDP growth from 0.2 percent in 1993 to 3.1 percent in 1996. Meanwhile, as a percent of GDP, the deficit rose from 2.44 percent to 4.99 percent, adding to public debt, which increased from 74.19 percent to 101.03 percent.

However, the timing of the VAT increase in April 1997, just prior to the East Asian financial crisis, likely exacerbated the effects of the crisis; and in 1999, after the largest drop in GDP growth since the 1950s, the government provided tax relief through temporary reductions in corporate and income taxes. This more expansionary approach to fiscal policy – intended to boost demand and support economic recovery – continued through October 2000. The resulting increase in the fiscal deficit (averaging 8.45 percent between 1998 and 2000) caused government debt to rise to 137.89 percent of GDP in 2000 – the highest among the G7 countries, the world's seven largest advanced economies, which include Canada, France, Germany, Italy, Japan, the United Kingdom, and the United States.

Monetary policy was also employed; but while low interest rates helped the government to manage its debt burden, they also caused tension in both the Japanese economy and society. Population aging meant that a large and growing segment – many financially reliant on income from saving – suffered low returns. Insurance companies and pension funds also suffered; and by 2001, six major insurers and more than one hundred pension plans – unable to meet payouts from their returns on investments – had collapsed.

From 2001 to 2006, the LDP administration of Junichiro Koizumi led the government; and fiscal reconstruction was re-established. The rising cost of maintaining the nonessential public facilities that had been built as part of earlier fiscal stimulus programs was widening the government's deficit – with a corresponding increase in public debt – causing concern about the sustainability of the fiscal balance. However, in response to the deterioration in macroeconomic performance in 2002, taxes were cut and the Bank of Japan opted for "quantitative easing" to return inflation to positive rates. As the economy started to recover, with GDP growth rising from 0.1 percent in 2002 to 2.2 percent in 2004, demand-side policies were replaced by "structural reforms" involving reconstruction of the supply-side of the economy, deregulation, and resolution of the bad loans problem. Between 2002 and 2007, smaller-scale countercyclical measures were implemented three times, while government budgets were consistently reduced, with the deficit falling from 8.05 percent in 2003 to 3.21 percent in 2007. But because the deficit had not been turned into a surplus, public debt increased further, from 162.73 percent to 175.43 percent of GDP during the same period.

Between Koizumi's resignation in 2006, and the LDP/New Komeito coalition led by Shinzo Abe coming to power in 2012, no government lasted much more than a year in office. However, there was a noticeable shift away from "small government" toward a "welfare state," as neoliberalism became less influential. Successive governments promoted work–life balance, established a National Council for Social Security, committed themselves to "strengthen[ing] the function of social security [but] constrain[ing] social security expenses," and proclaimed "peoples' life first."[16]

Following the 2008 collapse of Lehman Brothers, the Japanese government introduced a major expansion to counter the shock, maintaining an expanded budget to cope with the fallout of both the resulting world financial crisis and recession, as well as the East Japan earthquake, tsunami, and subsequent Fukushima Daiichi nuclear crisis of March 11, 2011.

Policy assessment

Japan has clearly not been without its speculative bubbles, but has relied far less on them for growth, by comparison to others. As a result, policy to either encourage them – or deal with the economic damage following their collapse – has also been less frequent, with policymakers typically taking a more stable, longer-term view and a countercyclical approach.

This had an influence on the development of the Japanese economy, which has not returned to its strong growth of the 1960s. However, the use of countercyclical fiscal and monetary policy – although it could probably have been more effectively coordinated – helped prevent deeper slumps. The use of austerity when the economy appeared to be recovering also minimized the contractionary effects of such policies. It is notable that in the fifty-six years since the early 1960s, the Japanese economy has only contracted in seven – and even then, by 1.2 percent or less in all but one.

Despite high (and growing) levels of public debt, which in 2017 reached nearly 240 percent of GDP – the highest in' the world – the yen has maintained its strength. Three key factors account for this: the government can service its debt without undue difficulty due to strong economic fundamentals; Japan has full control over its currency and a floating exchange rate; and most Japanese debt is held by its own citizens. These factors largely eliminate the possibility of austerity being enforced from abroad in the interests of foreign investors, rather than being a countercyclical policy, serving the Japanese economy and society.

Although Japan has suffered its "lost decade(s)" of slower economic growth – and more recently, growing poverty and unemployment, due to the neoliberal policies of the first half of the 2000s – its relatively homogeneous society, culture of teamwork, collective good, and treating people of all ages and needs fairly has so far helped to avoid the social breakdown experienced elsewhere. Japan has also managed to maintain social stability, harmony, and quality of life without the volatility that often accompanies a single-minded pursuit of economic growth – or austerity.

Conclusions

It is sometimes difficult to separate austerity from the rest of the policy package. In Pinochet's Chile, rather than eliminating public debt per se, austerity was a key tool in dismantling what was becoming a socialist state – and forcibly replacing it with its polar opposite. The removal of most of the welfare state certainly had the effect of rendering much of the Chilean population and workforce ineffective, while at the same time contributing to greatly increased poverty and inequality, with social, labor, and political push-back being suppressed by force.

Although, at the time, some pointed to data on growth and productivity in defense of the Chilean experiment, in reality, not only did Chile's economic performance lag behind that of its neighbors – then and ever since – but the growth and productivity figures used to justify austerity were significantly distorted by the reality that, after an extreme recession, the economy was recovering from an artificially low base. As with austerity itself, context is a key factor in interpreting data. The Chilean case is therefore simply one of many, where the data marshaled in support of austerity has been misleading. However, it is clear that an extreme version of austerity (in terms of extent and timescale) – allowed to run its full course through military backing – had no better economic outcomes than those interrupted by social and political opposition.

Events in America, under Reagan's targeted austerity, must also be seen in the context of the Cold War – which did little to play down the political dimensions of austerity across much of the Western world at the time. It is very clear that spending on military capability is usually seen very differently from that on welfare or infrastructure – as indeed it was when the concept of national debt first appeared three centuries ago. What is perhaps more surprising is that Reagan's administration was trying to justify austerity in welfare on the basis that both the deficit and debt needed reducing – while at the same time significantly increasing military spending. Political considerations clearly trumped economic strategy.

The question of the change in the proportion of US GDP devoted to welfare also underlines why economic growth is the best way of addressing both public deficits and debt; an increase in GDP growth will make the debt level suddenly look much smaller (based on the public debt-to-GDP ratio), even though its actual amount might remain unchanged. This also, as already discussed in the case of Chile's experiment with austerity, reminds us that data must be treated with some caution – and sometimes, skepticism.

The use of data is also a key factor in interpreting events in Ireland during the 1980s. The correlation between fiscal consolidation and economic growth was seen by some as evidence that austerity could actually be expansionary. But the Irish case does not confirm the theory of "expansionary fiscal consolidation." It does, however, provide a good example of trying to make the facts fit the theory (rather than the other way around). The reality of the Irish case comes down to the direction of causation – did austerity drive Ireland's expansion, or did economic growth provide the room for painless austerity? Given that Ireland's expansion preceded austerity, the evidence suggests that austerity is a necessary policy counterpart to stimulus, rather than being "expansionary" in its own right.

The Japanese case also casts doubt on the idea of a causal relationship between austerity and economic growth, but from a different perspective. Japan's debt has been very high for decades. But there is little sign of either hostile action by bond investors seen elsewhere – causing higher debt-servicing costs and a vicious cycle of increasing deficits and accumulated debt – or the economic stagnation predicted by Reinhard and Rogoff's 90 percent public debt-to-GDP threshold. The absence of hostile action can be largely explained by the fact that most Japanese debt is held by its own citizens; there is also little prospect that the means of funding the government's debt will be cut off. The Japanese case also adds to the accumulating evidence against the Reinhard and Rogoff thesis, since Japan has been operating quite effectively, well beyond the 90 percent debt threshold.

Overall, these cases suggest that austerity – even in its most extreme form – has not only failed to produce the predicted results; its timing and context are centrally important – in both economic policy and data interpretation.

7

Some Have Austerity Thrust Upon Them, Others Embrace It: Ireland, Greece, and Britain after the 2008 Crisis

Introduction

This chapter looks at three economies where severe austerity followed the 2008 financial crisis. Outwardly, the justification was the same – very high levels of public debt. However, from the point of view of both Ireland and Greece, the *actual* problem was the sudden loss of the means of financing that debt, rather than the amount of debt *per se*. Thus, while the stated aim was to reduce public debt, the real problem was finding other means of servicing it – which in the short term meant bailouts.

The UK also experienced higher than usual levels of public debt – the result, for the most part, of the combined cost of bank bailouts plus the cyclical deficit that accompanied a major recession. But unlike Greece or Ireland, Britain had no problems in servicing that debt. The UK has an independent currency and floating exchange rate – and therefore a range of financial strategy options. Nevertheless, austerity was implemented anyway, justified by two of the by now familiar arguments: first, the 90 percent public debt-to-GDP ratio had been exceeded; and second, the UK might become "another Greece" as a result of "loss of confidence in the currency." Since it is hard to see how either of these could *actually* afflict the UK – the first having been disproved both technically and by the experience of countries like Japan, and the second by the UK's full control over her currency – as we will see, another, more political reason, can be inferred.

But whatever the reason, all three countries were supposedly trying to reduce their debt burden; so it is against this objective that the success of their austerity policies must ultimately be judged.

Managing a Crisis: Austerity and Recovery in Ireland

The Irish economy appeared to perform well during the decade before the 2008 crisis. Between 1997 and 2007, annual GDP growth averaged 7.1 percent, with fiscal surpluses of 1.6 percent of GDP, permitting a steady reduction in the debt-to-GDP ratio, which fell from 70 percent to 24 percent. This had the political advantage of allowing governments to cut taxes, but still raise public spending, year-on-year.

However, with hindsight, this exceptionally strong macroeconomic performance was largely due to a credit boom, which fueled a real estate and construction bubble. When it burst, in 2007, the Irish banking system was seriously undermined, plunging the economy into a severe recession.

The bubble's origin can be traced to Ireland's 1999 entry into the Eurozone, which provided access to cheap finance from major European banks. Interest rates, set by the European Central Bank (ECB), amounted to zero (if not negative) real rates from 2000 onward. This powered a house-building boom and the quadrupling of house prices – making construction the dominant sector of the Irish economy. By 2007, it accounted for 13.3 percent of all employment – the highest in the OECD. However, the boom coincided with a drop in net exports, which, between 2002 and 2007, fell from 17 percent to 8 percent of GDP.

Policy aims

The 2008 financial crisis presented Ireland with two major problems. The first was the question of the stability – indeed survival – of its banking system; resolving this would undoubtedly increase national debt, which raised the second problem. By 2009, having lost the confidence of international investors, it was impossible to fund that debt through sovereign bonds. Since Ireland was now part of the Eurozone, it could not issue currency either; so any financial aid would involve the "Troika" (ECB, European Commission, and the IMF) – with austerity being a standard condition for assistance.

While reducing public debt was an important objective, the main aim was to restore the government's ability to fund its debt at an affordable cost – which meant regaining the confidence of the international investment community.

Policy development

The Irish housing bubble had been largely financed by its three main banks – Anglo Irish Bank, Allied Irish Banks, and Bank of Ireland – which prior to 2003 had operated in a very traditional manner, keeping loans roughly in line with deposits. However, the explosion in lending after 2003 was largely financed by bonds, issued to international investors; the banks also turned to the American wholesale money markets, typically borrowing overnight to fund thirty-year mortgages.

Even before 2007, although it was clear the banks were taking ever-greater risks – and that house prices were overvalued – the government and Central Bank did nothing to cool the market. Quite the opposite. The Central Bank actively promoted the financial services sector and its own "light touch" regulation; and during the 2007 election, political parties campaigned for abolition of stamp duty, which would have accelerated house price inflation even further. But by late 2007, demand for new houses collapsed, and prices dropped by half. This caused an abrupt shedding of construction jobs, raising the unemployment rate from 4.7 percent in 2007 to a peak of nearly 15 percent by 2012.

By 2008, the three main banks' combined assets amounted to 400 percent of GDP. As international investors became concerned about exposure to dubious property loans, the banks found it increasingly difficult to raise funds on the bond markets – and with the collapse of Lehman Brothers, effectively impossible. Unable to service their loans, they turned to the state. Fearing financial collapse, the government issued a two-year guarantee of almost all the Irish banking system's existing and future liabilities, in an attempt to convince the financial markets that the banks were sound.

As it became clear that such measures would not stop the banking crisis spilling over into the broader economy, the government set up the National Asset Management Agency (NAMA) to remove toxic assets from the banks' books. Using public money, NAMA bought these assets at above book value, selling shares in NAMA back to the banks, to be used as collateral to secure liquidity from the ECB.

Although Ireland's public finances now appeared to be in good shape, they were heavily dependent upon the health of the property sector. Thus, the collapse in construction brought a sharp drop in tax revenues and a major increase in unemployment-related welfare payments. The tax shortfall was made worse, by Ireland's tax base having been shifted away from income, toward taxes on construction, during the bubble. Years of budget surpluses were abruptly replaced by widening fiscal deficits, which increased from 7 percent of GDP in 2008 to over 32 percent in 2010.

The combination of large fiscal deficits and enormous bank bailout costs contributed to a rapid increase in the public debt-to-GDP ratio, which by 2010 was heading for 100 percent. With the collapse in construction and the world economy entering a severe recession, GDP contracted sharply, with growth of 5.2 percent in 2007 being replaced by contractions of 3.9 percent and 4.6 percent in 2008 and 2009, respectively.

From late 2008, in an effort to deal with its burgeoning public debt, the Irish government implemented contractionary budgets, including significant cuts in public sector pay, capital and non-welfare-related spending, as well as increases in income tax and VAT rates – the largest fiscal adjustments made by any advanced economy since the late 1970s. But austerity was not allowed to undermine either Ireland's social welfare system, or the state's redistributive mechanisms.

For a time, this seemed to restore confidence in Irish debt. But the nationalization of Anglo-Irish Bank in 2009 spooked investors, who worried that the banking sector might ultimately destroy the government's credit-worthiness. This triggered capital flight, which drained the Irish banks of the collateral required for ECB loans. So the ECB allowed the Irish Central Bank to extend "emergency liquidity assistance" loans. However, unable to raise funding from private capital markets, the government was forced to turn to the Troika for help, in return for which austerity was imposed.

The austerity measures fell into three main categories: fiscal consolidation, financial sector reforms, and structural labor market and protected sector reforms. Of those designed to reduce the budget deficit, one third were tax increases, with a large proportion coming from income; and the rest were cuts in capital development, public sector pay, and non-essential budget items.

Although many would pay significantly higher income taxes under the plan, a generous social welfare system and social protection schemes, as well as the redistributive arm of Ireland's fiscal policy, reduced the impact on the most vulnerable groups – probably sparing Ireland the social unrest experienced by other countries imposing austerity.

In the end, only the first two categories of the Troika's reform plan were effectively carried out. By 2013, the fiscal consolidation targets had been met, and the banking system had been both recapitalized and restructured, achieving the deleveraging target mainly by selling foreign assets. But very few structural reforms were carried out, since, by European standards, Ireland already had extensively deregulated markets.

There was also a reorientation of the economy back toward exports, which more than doubled between 2008 and 2011, from 8.6 percent to 18.7 percent of GDP, averaging 20 percent of GDP per year between 2009 and 2016. Export-oriented FDI inflows into Ireland were also strong, averaging 27 percent of GDP per year. Thus, the country's open, export-oriented economy, populated by multinationals, partially compensated for depressed domestic demand due to fiscal consolidation, lack of credit, and stressed household and business balance sheets. In 2010, there was a return to growth, which strengthened considerably after 2013, with GDP growing at 8.4 percent in 2014 and 5.1 percent by 2016.

Ireland has thus been considered a relative success story among the Eurozone's high-debt countries, improving market sentiment towards its sovereign debt, which – having peaked at 120 percent of GDP in 2012 – stood at 68 percent in 2017.

Policy assessment

It is hard to make a case for austerity being the driving force behind Ireland's recovery from the 2008 crisis. Although implementing contractionary budgets aimed at regaining market confidence, Ireland had also reoriented the economy toward key export industries and attracted further export-oriented FDI inflows. The government ensured that the cost of austerity was borne by those best able to cope, protecting vulnerable groups from the effects of both austerity and recession.

By 2010, as a result of this economic reorientation, growth had returned; so when Ireland was forced to turn to the Troika for assistance, the austerity measures coincided with significant growth, not recession. This meant that fiscal consolidation targets could be achieved while recapitalizing and restructuring the banking system. Although Ireland's public debt level remains high, having regained the confidence of international investors it is once again able to service that debt at an affordable rate – contributing to a virtuous cycle of budget surpluses and steady reductions in public debt.

Austerity in Greece: Made in Germany

Membership in the Eurozone brought mixed economic blessings for Greece. Prior to this, the Greek economy was characterized by relatively high inflation and interest rates, sluggish GDP growth, and significant fiscal and trade imbalances. But with its own currency, the drachma, state expenditure could be financed by expanding the money supply. While this effective devaluation discouraged overseas investment and undermined the value of domestic saving, it helped to keep both wages and the cost of exports low.

This state of affairs, however, was almost entirely reversed by Eurozone membership. Regular expansion of the money supply was no longer possible. But Greece was now able to borrow at the same low rates as economies such as Germany; and as a member of the Eurozone, Greek debt was considered less risky. So capital flooded in, much of it supplied by German banks. At the same time, though, the traditional Greek advantages of a flexible currency and low production costs were rapidly eroded. As a result, in the years leading up to the 2008 crisis, although annual Greek GDP growth averaged a more than laudable 4.2 percent, this masked some serious problems. Between 2001 and 2009, Greece's competitiveness deteriorated by around 30 percent; and the government's deficit significantly increased (from 5.5 percent to 15.1 percent of GDP), with a corresponding rise in the public debt-to-GDP ratio (from 107.1 percent to 126.7 percent).

This situation might well have proved unsustainable in the longer term. But Greece suddenly found herself in difficulty because of the combination of the financial crisis, the "Great Recession," and the revelation that – with the help of US banks, including Goldman Sachs – Greece had been masking the true level of its debts through various accounting mechanisms that circumvented Eurostat rules. As a result, existing concerns about debt on the part of the freshly bailed-out financial markets – a problem caused by the cost of those bailouts – were rapidly ratcheted-up. Market confidence collapsed, increasing Greece's cost of borrowing, which rose from around 4 percent to 40 percent. This caused the government's deficit and debt to increase at a still faster pace, making it increasingly impossible to service.

The triggers for the introduction of austerity were thus excessive national debt, the undermining of confidence in the government's ability to avoid a sovereign debt default, and loss of confidence in the currency. However, in this case, that currency was not Greece's own, but the euro. With no common fiscal policy in the Eurozone, there were few mechanisms in place to deal with such a crisis; and following the more gentle austerity initially imposed by the Greek government, the rest would be dictated by the Troika. Greek politicians and economists would thus have progressively less influence over Greek public policy.

Policy aims

From the brief summary above, a number of policy aims in addressing the Greek crisis can be surmised. The first was to ensure that the crisis remained a "Greek" crisis, rather than spreading to other Eurozone economies in not dissimilar situations – for not dissimilar reasons. This would involve convincing the financial markets that the situation in Greece was under control – and that there was no need to reassess the sovereign debt risk profiles of Portugal, Italy, Ireland, and Spain, which, together with Greece, were collectively (and unkindly) referred to as the "PIIGS" – a situation that would have made the crisis much larger (and, quite possibly, uncontrollable).

Second was the question of the exposure of German and other Eurozone banks to the large amounts of (highly leveraged) Greek debt they held. A sharp increase in the borrowing costs of the PIIGS was not the only threat to the credibility – or indeed viability – of the euro. A major sovereign debt default by Athens could have a very significant impact on Europe's banking system and, by extension, the currency itself. To address this – and allow those banks involved to unwind their exposure – would take time. This would mean not only bolstering market confidence, but also encouraging Greece to stay in the Eurozone – for the time being, at least – and resisting any calls for forgiving significant portions of Greek debt. All of this suggested that austerity – for many years, a condition for support from the IMF – would play a significant part in the Troika's response.

Policy development

The first austerity measures – introduced in December 2009 by the newly elected Panhellenic Socialist Movement (Pasok) government, and significantly expanded in early 2010 – were met with mass protests and strikes. But it became apparent that any savings from these initial cuts to the public sector would be too little, too late, to stop continually rising debt servicing costs driving up both the deficit and the national debt – and further eroding market confidence. Without access to market funding at affordable rates or control over its currency, Greece had no choice but to seek a bailout.

By 2010, it was also clear that the Maastricht Eurozone stability criteria had been significantly exceeded. Annual fiscal deficits were officially capped at 3 percent of GDP, but Greece had reached 15.1 percent by the end of 2009, with a national debt of 126.9 percent of GDP – more than double the maximum Eurozone ratio of 60 percent. In May, fears of a Greek sovereign debt default prompted approval of the Troika's first bailout of €110 billion ($147 billion). This fended-off default by covering the cost of maturing bonds. But it came at the cost of stringent austerity measures, structural reforms, and the privatization of much of the Greek public sector, which led to a general strike, widespread protests, and political upheaval. Meanwhile, being imposed during a deep recession, the austerity package simply made the slump worse – creating the need for a second bailout.

In July 2011, EU leaders agreed a bailout of €109 billion ($157 billion) from the European Financial Stability Facility. By now, voluntary debt relief by private creditors was also on the agenda – of senior German politicians, at least – since it was becoming apparent that the fragile Greek economy was struggling to keep-up with the repayments. However, both Jean-Claude Trichet, then President of the ECB, and private finance, generally, feared the effect of a significant "haircut" for private bondholders on a banking system already weakened by the 2008 crisis. Nevertheless, a significant writedown was finally agreed, with private bondholders accepting extended maturities, lower rates, and a reduction of 53.5 percent in the Greek bonds' base value – in return for further austerity measures. The Greek Prime Minister George Papandreou announced a referendum on the rescue package, but withdrew it shortly afterwards and resigned, being replaced by an interim Prime Minister, Lucas Papademos, former head of the Bank of Greece.

This paved the way for the second Troika bailout, ratified in February 2012, against a backdrop of violent protests against the latest tough austerity measures. The bailout, worth €130 billion ($173 billion), included €48 billion for recapitalizing the four largest Greek banks, justified by the argument that this was economically superior to nationalizing and reforming them.

This was followed by what appeared (for some) to be a light at the end of the tunnel, when the Greek government predicted a structural surplus for 2014. Greek access to the private bond markets was briefly reopened, helping to finance that year's deficit. But hope proved short-lived, with the rapidly shrinking Greek economy mired in recession, more than a quarter of the labor force unemployed, the government continuing to run a deficit, and the 2014 debt-to-GDP ratio rising to 178.9 percent.

The 2015 elections saw the anti-austerity Syriza party's leader Alexis Tsipras elected Prime Minister and forming a coalition government with the nationalist Independent Greeks Party. In February, having again been locked out of the international financial markets, the new government negotiated a four-month extension to the Troika's bailout. In return, it was forced to abandon its promised anti-austerity measures and undertake further reforms. But on 26 June, Tsipras announced a referendum on austerity.

That same day, a report by the IMF revealed that Greece's "debt dynamics" were "unsustainable," making the case that debt reduction would be required for Greece to be able to repay its debts. The IMF, which played a central role in monitoring rescue packages – and is forbidden to lend to countries it deems insolvent – therefore refused to support a third Troika bailout unless Greece was granted debt relief. On June 30, Greece missed its scheduled €1.5 billion ($1.7 billion) payment, the first time an advanced economy had defaulted on a loan repayment to the IMF.

On 6 July, Greek voters overwhelmingly rejected the bailout terms (61 percent to 39 percent, with 62.5 percent voter turnout). But despite this, on July 15, the Greek parliament passed further austerity measures in an effort to secure another bailout that would help avoid bankruptcy and an exit from the Eurozone. Eurozone leaders provisionally agreed another EU loan of €86 billion ($95 billion) over the next three years, which would allow Greece to make payments on its existing debt.

This third bailout was ratified by the Greek parliament on August 14, with the first payment being received on August 19. The loan was conditional on achieving a target primary surplus – which excludes the cost of debt financing – of 3.5 percent of GDP by 2018, plus further privatization, reforms of the tax and pension systems, and liberalization of the Greek economy and labor market.

Tsipras won a snap election in September, giving him the electoral mandate to push for debt relief in negotiations with the EU. But he persisted with the Troika's austerity measures and structural reforms. Thus, in spite of the 2015 elections producing a sharp move to the left, a Syriza government led by Tsipras, and a referendum result that clearly rejected the idea of any further austerity, remarkably little changed in the pattern of bailouts and austerity – which only led to continuing recession and social problems.

Discussions about debt relief continued. But Germany's Chancellor Angela Merkel and Finance Minister Wolfgang Schäuble steadfastly resisted the idea; and in May 2016, it was agreed to postpone any Greek debt relief until the fall of 2018, after Greece had exited the third and final bailout. The stalemate between the IMF and EU creditors extended into 2017 when, in June, the IMF announced that it would formally join the third Troika bailout – but not release any funds until after the Europeans spelled out what kind of debt relief they would accept. The IMF would also undertake enhanced surveillance and monitor Greece's fiscal discipline and adherence to the bailout conditions.

In September, Merkel secured a fourth term in office, but with significantly reduced authority. Her party, the Christian Democratic Union of Germany (CDU) posted its worst result since 1949 – losing sixty-five seats in the Bundestag – while the radical right-wing (nationalist and populist) Alternative for Germany (AfD) became the third largest party, and the pro-business Free Democratic Party (FDP) returned to parliament as the fourth. Schäuble's resignation also made future negotiations about debt relief that much more likely.

In late 2017, another light appeared at the end of the tunnel when Greece posted both its first primary surplus in memory – and GDP growth of 1.4 percent. But business confidence continued to fall, while public discontent over the government's failed pledge to end austerity remained high.

In January 2018, the Greek parliament agreed yet more austerity measures to qualify for the next round of bailout payments; and at the end of June, nineteen Eurozone finance ministers announced the end of the eight-year-long Greek debt crisis. But they refused to write off any Greek debt, agreeing instead to extend and defer repayments of €320 billion ($370 billion), due to begin in 2022, until 2032. The deal also provides a "cash buffer" of €24 billion ($28 billion) – the final €15 billion tranche of the €86 billion bailout plus an extra €9 billion – to cover Greece's sovereign financial needs for the next twenty-two months, plus any profits the ECB realizes on its holdings of Greek bonds. In exchange, Greece must implement even more austerity (through additional taxes and pension cuts), maintain a primary budget surplus of 3.5 percent of GDP until 2022, and a target surplus of 2.2 percent through 2060.

Policy assessment

Overall, Greece was tasked with the largest fiscal consolidation of any Eurozone economy following the 2008 financial crisis. The side effects of this – notably a sharply negative impact on the already parlous public debt-to-GDP ratio – took even the IMF by surprise. But perhaps the most significant development was that the IMF's participation in the third Troika bailout was contingent on significant debt relief, due to its belief that, by 2015, the level of Greek debt was unsustainable, even after six years of bailouts, austerity, and restructuring. The IMF's stance on debt relief was at odds with countries like Germany, which had purchased significant volumes of Greek bonds and resisted discussing possible debt relief until early 2018. But at the time of writing, there has been no cancellation of Greek debt, beyond the haircut accepted by private bondholders in 2011.

While the Greek sovereign debt crisis was declared "over" in the second quarter of 2018, the question of whether the policy response to it has been successful is rather more complex. True, banking systems across Europe survived without further major damage; and a currency crisis in the Eurozone was averted. However, both of these outcomes were the result of the extensive bailout funds, not austerity policy.

From the point of view of those demanding austerity, Greece's economic and social problems came largely without political cost. Only in Greece was there a major political penalty, with the PASOK party (Panhellenic Socialist Movement), which oversaw the first two years of austerity, paying the price – and ultimately being unseated by the more left-wing Syriza movement, elected on an anti-austerity platform. It remains to be seen whether Syriza will suffer a similar fate at the hands of the electorate. In spite of a very significant reduction in living conditions in Greece, with many slipping into poverty and homelessness, widespread protests and rioting, plus an ongoing migration crisis, Tsipras, found himself unable to resist the austerity measures demanded to unlock bailout funds, and avoid default and Eurozone exit.

But very little of those bailout funds – 95 percent of which flowed straight back out of the Greek economy to pay creditors – was used to help the Greek economy recover and develop to a point where its debt load could be regarded as manageable. The deep and sustained austerity programs, however, had predictable effects. Between 2008 and 2016, unemployment more than tripled, from 7.8 percent to 23.5 percent, having peaked in 2013 at 27.5 percent – with youth unemployment around twice that. GDP growth contracted sharply, averaging an annual decline of 3.6 percent; and the economy shrunk by more than a quarter. The Greek state also contracted, with public sector employment dropping by over a quarter, and incomes falling by 40 percent. Government expenditure was reduced by an average annual rate of 3.6 percent between 2010 and 2016, mostly the result of large reductions in pensions, healthcare, and social welfare programs, which together were cut by 70 percent.

The austerity demands also resulted in the selling-off of most of Greece's national assets. Market liberalization caused one in three small businesses to go bankrupt; labor market reforms drove down wages and increased precarious employment. However, from 2019, pensions are to be further reduced, taxes raised, and labor market reforms will suspend the ban on mass dismissals, comprehensive collective bargaining, and industrial action – reforms that are incompatible with the European Charter of Fundamental Rights, which guarantees these rights.

Predictably, despite the extreme austerity and structural reforms, between 2009 and 2015, the government's deficit remained stubbornly high – averaging 12.7 percent of GDP – before it turned into a small surplus of 0.6 percent of (a significantly lower) GDP in 2016 and 0.8 percent in 2017. The level of Greece's national debt, however, remains extremely high, at 178.6 percent of GDP in 2017, with no significant economic growth or trade surplus to help pay it off.

Perhaps the biggest question about Greece's ability to generate the economic resources that will be required to repay its debt is the structure of its economy. Services have overtaken all other sectors, accounting for around 80 percent of GDP, with the public sector representing 40 percent and tourism representing 18 percent. The average size of Greek businesses remains small and many have fallen victim to the prolonged recession. Thus, although fiscal targets were technically reached, the Greek private sector has been very seriously impaired.

As a member of the Eurozone – and in the absence of a fiscal union – it is difficult to see how Greece can significantly reduce its debt without considerable debt forgiveness by its creditors. Its future is thus unclear, as suggested by the IMF's June 29, 2018 *Concluding Statement*, following an official visit: "The debt relief recently agreed with Greece's European partners has significantly improved debt sustainability over the medium-term, but longer-term prospects remain uncertain."[1]

In short, while the bailouts could be seen as a financial success for the Eurozone – and the banks that had extended loans to Greece – the accompanying program of austerity has failed to improve the Greek economy; and in many respects it has undermined Greece's ability to generate the GDP growth necessary for debt reduction.

Austerity in Post-2008 Britain: Economics or Politics?

At the time of writing, eight years after the turn to austerity in 2010, the United Kingdom's recovery from the recession precipitated by the 2008 financial crisis is not only the deepest and longest in almost a century; it is also the slowest in recorded history.

The initial response – emergency bank recapitalization and fiscal and monetary stimulus – was undertaken by Gordon Brown's Labour government. It was relatively successful in dealing with what was then understood to be a crisis of growth. After a drop in GDP growth – from 2.4 percent in 2007 to contractions of 0.5 percent in 2008 and 4.2 percent in 2009

– by 2010, a weak recovery was under way. However, "market" concerns about both rising government deficits (which increased from 2.6 percent of GDP in 2007 to 10.1 percent in 2009) and high levels of public debt (which rose from 41.9 percent to 64.1 percent of GDP during the same period) soon motivated a reinterpretation of the crisis – as one of "debt," rather than "growth."[2]

It was claimed that investors in government bonds were worried about an increased risk of default – supported by events in Greece and the weaker Eurozone economies at the time. Unless government deficits and debt were reduced, it was argued, the cost of borrowing would increase, widening the deficit and, as a result, increasing debt. Thus, even though the UK has control over its currency and a floating exchange rate – and is therefore in no *actual* danger of defaulting on her debt – "the politics of austerity took over."[3]

Policy aims

In this instance, it is difficult to be certain whether the stated objectives of austerity – elimination of the government's deficit and debt – were in fact the primary ones. While the UK state sector had indeed expanded somewhat under Tony Blair's New Labour, the principle causes of the increased deficit and debt after 2008 could hardly be more obvious – bank bailouts and emergency stimulus combined with reduced tax revenues and higher social welfare costs triggered by the recession. As a result, the reinterpretation of the cause of the crisis strongly suggests that a reduction in the size of the state might also have been an objective.

Policy development

Whatever the true motivation, in 2009, the term "age of austerity" – previously used to describe the years immediately following World War I – was popularized by the then Conservative Party leader David Cameron. In a speech to the Conservative Party Forum, he declared that "the age of irresponsibility is giving way to the age of austerity," pledging to end excessive government spending if elected in the following year's general election.

The tone for the election was set in an open letter to *The Sunday Times*, signed by twenty economists from so-called "top universities," admonishing the Labour government for inadequate efforts at deficit reduction: "In order to be credible, the government's goal should be to eliminate the structural current deficit" – the part of a deficit that remains after growth has returned to normal – "over the course of a parliament."[4] In debates preceding the election, however, Brown rejected spending cuts because, in his view, they would make the recession worse. Nick Clegg, then leader of the Liberal Democrats, branded budget cuts "economic masochism." Only Cameron pledged to cut public expenditure – but did not elaborate on precisely how.

The election produced a Conservative–Liberal Democrat coalition, with Clegg now claiming that he had changed his mind about spending cuts before the election. So in a major policy reversal, he abandoned commitment to stimulus and backed the Conservatives' austerity plan.

In June 2010, the new Chancellor, George Osborne, officially defined the crisis as one of debt, telling the House of Commons that "unless we deal with our debts, there will be no growth." He then announced a £40 billion "emergency" austerity budget involving tax increases (including VAT) and cuts in social welfare, with the aim of eliminating the structural deficit and reducing public debt by the end of the 2015 parliamentary session.

At the 2011 Conservative Party Conference, Cameron reiterated his commitment to austerity:

> This was no normal recession: we're in a debt crisis. It was caused by too much borrowing, by individuals, businesses, banks, and most of all, governments … The only way out of a debt crisis is to deal with your debts. That's why households are paying down their credit card and store card bills. It means banks getting their books in order. And it means governments – all over the world – cutting spending and living within their means."[5]

But instead of boosting the recovery, austerity slowed it down; and in another blow to the idea of "expansionary austerity," the promised private sector-led expansion failed to materialize.

Between 2010 and 2012, GDP growth stagnated, at well below 2 percent, while unemployment remained stubbornly high at around 8 percent (compared with pre-crisis rates of about 5 percent). Due to continuing deficits, public debt increased, reaching 84.5 percent of GDP in 2012.

In response, the *New Statesman*, under the headline "How to Lose Friends and Alienate Economists," went back to *The Sunday Times*'s twenty economists to ask whether they still stood by what they had said in 2010. Only one still did; the rest denied their earlier error of judgement, claiming that they no longer held the same view, given "changed circumstances."

Later that year, the austerity program – which in practice involved a sharp reduction in the *rate of increase* in public expenditure (as opposed to an absolute reduction) – was quietly relaxed.[6] However, the political rhetoric continued; and by 2013, all three main parties endorsed deficit reduction as the central component of fiscal policy.

In a 2013 speech, Cameron argued that public spending reductions should be permanent – as a means of making the state "leaner, not just now, but permanently" – and that he had no intention of increasing spending, even after the structural deficit had been eliminated. This went on record as having the objective of reducing the size and economic role of the state. The following year, the Treasury extended the proposed austerity period until at least 2018, with the Labour Shadow Chancellor, Ed Balls, in a speech to the Fabian Society, adding his own party's commitment to austerity:

> Without fiscal discipline and a credible commitment to eliminate the deficit, we cannot achieve the stability we need ... Labour will combine iron discipline on spending control and action on growth, with a fairer approach to deficit reduction. That means facing up to the tough choices that are necessary if we are to take a fairer approach to deficit reduction.[7]

By the end of the 2015 parliamentary session, the government had failed to eliminate the deficit – by a wide margin. Instead, economic growth had been reduced, averaging only 2 percent per year, compared with 2.6 percent between 1948 and 2007. Although the deficit as a percent of GDP had been reduced to 4.3 percent (less than half of its level in 2010), it was still a deficit. So while the sale of government assets (mostly shares of stock in the nationalized banks) had slowed the rate of increase in public debt, which stood at 88.2 percent of GDP in 2010, it was 17 percent higher than it had been when the coalition came to power.

Unsurprisingly, then, public deficits and debt, including who was responsible for them and further plans for reducing them – were major campaign issues in the 2015 general election. While the smaller parties (Plaid Cymru, the Greens, and the Scottish National Party (SNP)) opposed austerity, the Conservatives, Labour, Lib Dems, and United Kingdom Independence Party (UKIP) all supported it.

The economy however, wasn't the only major campaign issue. The question of continued membership in the European Union also loomed large as, in 2013, under pressure from many of his MPs and UKIP, Cameron had announced that, if elected, a Conservative government would hold an in–out referendum before the end of 2017.

The Conservatives won the election outright, after which Clegg, Labour leader Ed Miliband, and UKIP leader Nigel Farage all resigned as leaders of their respective parties. The Labour Party, driven by popular (rather than political) pressure, moved perceptively to the left, electing Jeremy Corbyn, who was unambiguously anti-austerity – supported by many who felt that they had been negatively affected by previous spending cuts.

In 2016, Cameron announced that the referendum on continued EU membership would indeed take place. The surprise outcome in favor of leaving the EU resulted in Cameron's resignation and, shortly afterwards, Osborne's removal by the incoming Prime Minister Theresa May. Just like that, the two key political proponents of austerity left office – although austerity would prove to have more staying power.

May called for an early general election in 2017, in the hope of securing a stronger electoral mandate for her Brexit negotiations. Although her campaign hinted at a shift to a more caring "one-nation conservativism," its focus was firmly on May's authority as Prime Minister. By contrast, Labour's campaign focused on ending austerity as well as on policies for strengthening both the economy and social welfare state.

As it turned out, the Labour Party position on austerity had far more resonance with voters than had been supposed, putting the party within reach of government by increasing its share of the vote from 30.4 percent to 40.0 percent. May's bid for a better negotiating hand with the EU was one of the casualties of this strong performance. Having lost the Conservative majority, she would now be leading a minority government.

However, despite the clear message from voters in relation to austerity, in a speech at Mansion House, Philip Hammond, Osborne's replacement as Chancellor, confirmed that austerity would continue until the deficit – which in 2017 stood at 1.9 percent of GDP – had been cleared. Public debt also remained stubbornly high, at 87.7 percent of GDP.

At the 2018 Conservative Party Conference, May appeared to shift course when she took the party by surprise and pledged to "end" austerity; and shortly afterward, Hammond announced that a "good" Brexit deal would "pave the way" for this. But at the time of writing, it seems more likely that "ending" austerity *actually* means "calling it something else."

Policy assessment

Taking the government's original stated objectives of austerity at face value, it is very difficult to describe the UK's austerity program as a success. While the deficit was reduced, it was not turned to surplus – so public debt continued to rise. It is also worth noting that economic growth would most likely have been strengthened without the drag of austerity; and stronger growth would have resulted in a larger and faster reduction in the deficit. Add to this that the government's program of austerity directly contributed to the rise of a newly energized – and decidedly more left-wing – Labour Party, the outcome, from a Conservative Party perspective, looks very poor indeed.

Following the 2008 crisis, the initial sharp rise in both the government's deficit and its debt was, even on a cursory examination, caused by cyclical rather than structural factors, with obvious contributors being the bank bailouts, emergency stimulus, and automatic stabilizers triggered by the recession. The best solution to rising public deficits and debt might well have been to simply let the cyclical component of the cycle run its course, perhaps with the odd economic "nudge." But this is to ignore the political dimension of austerity. If smaller government was indeed one of the Conservative Party's austerity policy objectives – as it clearly was, based on Cameron's 2013 speech – then the policies of the last eight years might be considered somewhat more successful. The evidence is undisputable: government spending as a percent of GDP fell steadily, from a peak of 21.6 percent in 2009 to 18.4 percent in 2017, as did public sector employment, from 22.1 percent to 17.0 percent of total employment. Yet even here, there is the question of what effect any future Labour government might have on the size and role of the state – a possibility that is significantly more likely following the electorate's response to the social and economic impact of sustained austerity.

Conclusions

Like the banks before the 2008 financial crisis, Ireland and Greece appeared to be doing very well in terms of GDP growth – until suddenly they weren't. Both countries were undone by similar forces to those behind the 2008 financial crisis: irresponsible lending at low rates of interest and high levels of leverage, followed by an interruption in the flow of cheap credit. It is essential to bear this in mind, as the national bailouts that followed were primarily aimed at keeping the payments flowing to creditors – thus protecting the euro – rather than addressing the actual levels of public debt.

Both Ireland and Greece still have extremely high levels of debt – austerity having made little, if any, impact. Creditors, however, have concluded that "the crisis is over" in both cases, mostly because (for now, at least) payments are flowing again, without further bailouts. However, Ireland's recovery has been much stronger than that of Greece due to the basic structure of its economy. Its high value-added, export-oriented industries are effective drivers of growth, helping to service the government's debt. By contrast, Greece's recovery (if it exists at all) is very fragile; its economy has no real industrial base, being dependent on relatively low value-added sectors, like public services and tourism.

The UK case shows that while a strong expansion can certainly support austerity, austerity can easily choke off a weak one. This is exactly what happened after 2010. True, the real aims of the government's austerity policies might well have been different from those originally stated. But the stated objectives were not only the usual ones (reducing government deficits and debt); they also had the predictable results. When austerity failed to reverse Britain's public deficit, debt kept rising, with the deficit position only strengthening through a return to modest growth.

Austerity – in the absence of protections for the most vulnerable groups within society – also had the usual social and political effects. In Britain and Greece, austerity contributed to high and rising unemployment, poverty, and inequality – creating social pressure and significant political shifts. The British Labour Party moved decisively to the left, while, in Greece, Syriza rose to power. While politicians and media alike claimed to be surprised by all of this, they shouldn't have been. As we've already seen, the experience of Weimar Germany demonstrates what can happen when the means of funding debt-fueled growth is cut off, while austerity during a recession has a long history of making things worse – which, in turn, has usually produced strong nationalist pressure for social and political change.

Overall, in all three cases, austerity failed against its stated objectives. In Greece and the UK, public debt is the same or higher than it was when austerity policies were first implemented; and in Ireland, public debt was reduced, not by austerity, but by strong GDP growth, which, in turn, made debt reduction possible.

8
Post-2008 Variations on Austerity: Iceland and America

Introduction

Iceland and the United States were both in the front line of the 2008 financial crisis; and they faced similar problems to the previous cases, including recession, increased debt, and devastated financial systems. But while both also implemented austerity, they did so during a sustainable recovery – and even then, only as a very minor part of the policy mix. Compared with countries that chose austerity as a core policy, with or without bailouts, the American and Icelandic economies recovered more quickly – and strongly.

Having a sovereign currency was another factor in the two cases, providing much more scope for choosing alternative policies to austerity. In the case of Iceland, not being a member of the European Union meant that, in seeking emergency assistance, it dealt with the IMF (rather than the Troika), which allowed austerity to be postponed until growth had been restored. This, together with observation of the experience of other EU member states, subject to the Troika's involvement in emergency support, had the effect of reversing Icelandic public opinion on EU membership, which had previously been overwhelmingly in favor of joining.

In both cases, culture also played a part in the government's response. In the US, the Great Depression – and the New Deal that helped address it – remains a vivid part of America's cultural history. These memories would influence the initial response to the crisis, in particular, with calls for spending cuts coming only after political change – and once the initial fear had passed. In Iceland, too, culture played a role. A tight-knit community, society was put firmly ahead of both finance and ideology – whether political or economic.

Iceland: Putting Society Ahead of Finance

By 2017, the Icelandic economy – which had been at the epicenter of the 2008 financial crisis – was instead the fastest growing in the OECD, powered by rising incomes and profits rather than leverage. Iceland also recorded the highest levels of equality in both income and gender balance, the lowest level of poverty, the highest union density, and living standards exceeding pre-crisis levels. Private debt had been greatly reduced; and government debt was falling rapidly, as were interest payments, creating the fiscal space to address spending needs. Inflation was below 2.5 percent; and the current account and government fiscal balances were both in surplus. Even net investment had turned positive for the first time.

Iceland's three largest banks (Arion, formerly Kaupthing; Islandsbanki, formerly Glitnir; and Landsbankinn, formerly Landsbanki) – which had been allowed to fail in 2008 (with combined assets amounting to almost ten times the country's GDP) – were also performing well. They were well capitalized, with a combined capital ratio far above the regulatory minimum, and high by international standards. Capital controls, introduced during the crisis, had been largely dismantled; and a new regulatory framework governing capital flows had been put in place.

Policy aims

Although Iceland has been the "poster child" for *not* turning to austerity following the 2008 crisis, the country's remarkable recovery is rather more complex, with a varied policy mix – including austerity. However, austerity measures were *not* part of the primary response; and they were focused on sectors *other* than social welfare, with tax increases being borne by the wealthy.

Policy development

Between 1991 and 2004, Iceland had adopted major market-oriented reforms, including cuts in government spending, reductions in corporate and income tax rates, privatization of state-owned enterprises, and closer integration into global markets. In 1994, it joined the European Economic Area (EEA), the free-trade bloc of the EU, which gave it access to European markets. The country's business and political leaders were also quick to recognize the profit-making potential of a privatized, deregulated, and expanded financial services sector; and from the late 1990s, Icelandic banks were privatized and the financial sector deregulated in a highly politicized process, completed in 2003.

The ensuing finance-driven growth was aided by the Central Bank of Iceland's (CBI) policy of hiking interest rates to manage inflation. As the differential between Icelandic and international rates increased, financial traders profited by borrowing at lower interest rates outside Iceland, and then lending in Iceland at the higher rate. Foreign banks bought Icelandic bonds and repackaged them, selling them on as "glacier bonds," with interest rates up to five times those of other European bonds. The inflow of money pushed up the value of the krona relative to other world currencies, encouraging Icelanders to spend more on what were now relatively inexpensive imports.

Between 2003 and 2007, real estate speculation saw house prices rise by an average annual rate of 16.6 percent. This was supported by virtually unlimited credit, since all citizens had equal access to the Housing Financing Fund (HFF), a government institution formed in 1999 to provide low interest mortgages. By 2004, almost 90 percent of Icelandic households held an HFF loan, while HFF-issued bonds made up more than half the Icelandic bond market. Meanwhile, the banks' acquisition of businesses at home and abroad fueled a stock market bubble, with annual share price appreciation averaging 43.7 percent. Booming housing and stock markets generated an increase in both corporate and household wealth, which encouraged further borrowing and spending, adding to GDP growth. However, they also caused a sharp deterioration in the trade imbalance, with the current account deficit rising from 5 percent of GDP in 2003 to 25 percent in 2008. Market liberalization and financialization also brought a rapid increase in inequality, with the Gini coefficient rising from 0.24 in 2003 to a peak of 0.30 in 2008,[1] while the share of the top 1 percent in gross income rose from 5.43 percent in 1992 to a peak of 19.75 percent in 2007. Poverty also increased, with 10.2 percent of households having disposable incomes of less than 60 percent of the median by 2008.

Nevertheless, between 2003 and 2008, fueled by the highly leveraged expansion of its leading banks, Iceland's annual GDP growth averaged 6.3 percent. Between them, the banks' assets increased from less than twice national GDP in 2003, to over eight times in 2007 and almost ten times by June 2008 – making it impossible for them to be rescued by the government in the event of trouble.

In September 2008, trouble – in the form of the collapse of Lehman Brothers – arrived, triggering a freezing-up of international credit markets. Iceland's three major banks failed and were taken over by the Icelandic government, leading to a succession of interrelated crises in the currency, stock, housing, and debt repayment markets. The krona depreciated by over 80 percent against the euro, while the stock market lost 75 percent of its value. Real wages fell by 4.2 percent in 2008 and another 8 percent in 2009; unemployment reached 7.2 percent in 2009, while GDP fell by 6.9 percent.

Iceland was now facing the "nightmare scenario" that many Western economies had sought to avoid, by resorting to bank bailouts, emergency stimulus, and, in more than a few cases, significant austerity. But Iceland could not simply focus on one thing, such as its debt, because it had far too many problems for that. So a much wider approach was required. Following the collapse of the party in government during the crisis and the early responses to it, the general thrust of the approach was simple: Iceland's future as a society mattered far more to Iceland than the money did. This would be the guiding idea for dealing with an apparently intractable and generalized crisis.

Strict capital controls, including the temporary suspension of the official currency exchange, were introduced to help both protect the currency and avoid a widespread default on household and corporate debts. The government then turned to the IMF for an emergency loan; and on October 24, a package totaling $2.1 billion was announced under the IMF's fast-track emergency financing mechanism. The executive board approved the two-year stand-by agreement, making $827 million available immediately, with the remainder to be paid in eight equal instalments, subject to quarterly review. Bilateral funding of $3 billion was also provided by the Faroe Islands, Nordic countries, and Poland.

In exchange for these loans, the Icelandic government made a commitment to both reduce public spending and honor its obligations to insured foreign depositors in the failed banks. But crucially, the IMF did *not* require austerity until the recession had bottomed out. Meanwhile, the banks were restructured, new boards and management were appointed, and a more effective banking regulatory framework was set up. Each bank was split into two, with the new state-owned banks servicing domestic banking needs, and the old banks dealing with international obligations.

However, Iceland's population had lost faith in conventional politics, holding weekly protests outside parliament over the government's role in the crisis – and its subsequent handling of it. The protests intensified until the government collapsed, at which point a coalition of the Alliance Party and the Left-Green Movement took over on an interim basis, before being elected to govern in April 2009.

The new government pledged to take a Nordic-style welfare approach, sheltering lower- and middle-income groups against the worst effects of the crisis. This also had implications for the form that the IMF-requested austerity would eventually take. The government aimed to safeguard the welfare state against cuts, with austerity being focused on other sectors. There were limited tax reductions for working-class citizens, but increased taxes for higher-income groups. Household and non-financial business debt was reduced by restructuring, write-offs, and relief. Improvements were made to old-age pensions, disability benefits, social assistance allowances, unemployment benefits, and the minimum wage. The government also wrote off the mortgage debts of a quarter of the population and introduced rent rebates to help those in rented accommodation.

By sheltering the more vulnerable groups, the trend toward increasing inequality was reversed in 2008 and 2009. From its peak of 0.30 in 2008, the Gini coefficient dropped to 0.24 in 2013, where it remained in 2015. The poverty rate also declined, with the proportion of households with disposable income below 60 percent of the median falling from 10.2 percent in 2008 to 7.9 percent in 2011. The share of the top 1 percent in gross income, which had peaked in 2007 at 19.75 percent, stood at 7.92 percent by 2015.

In June 2009, under pressure from the IMF, as well as from the UK and Netherlands – which had reimbursed their depositors when the Icelandic internet-based banking service "Icesave" collapsed – the Icelandic government agreed to repay the debt. Parliament approved a bill detailing the repayment schedule, but the UK and Netherlands rejected the terms, with an amended bill based on more stringent terms being approved in December. However, popular pressure forced President Ólafur Ragnar Grímsson to hold a referendum, in which 93 percent of Icelanders rejected both the proposals and the idea that the people (rather than bankers and business leaders) should pay back the debt. The European Free Trade Association (EFTA) Surveillance Authority subsequently sued Iceland in the EFTA court, which decided the case in Iceland's favor.

In 2012, legal proceedings were launched against Geir Haarde, the former Prime Minister, who was found guilty of breaking the law on the responsibility of ministers. Senior bank management, as well as business leaders, also faced charges relating to fraud and manipulation.

By 2013, although growth had returned and unemployment had fallen to 5.4 percent, inflation (caused by the devalued krona) was depressing real earnings, investment was low, and the state was still in deep debt. About 15 percent of households were also having difficulty making ends meet; and despite the introduction of new programs for the unemployed, and the strengthening of existing ones, there were few new jobs. There was also little trust in Iceland's parliament, the CBI, and the City Council of the capital city, Reykjavic.

Thus, although the 2009 coalition government had delivered on most of its promises, elections in 2013 brought a new coalition of the two center-right opposition parties. But the reforms begun by the 2009–13 coalition government continued apace. In October 2015, six months ahead of schedule

– having already repaid the bilateral loans – Iceland repaid the IMF emergency loan. By this time, the economy had largely recovered, being much more diversified and less dependent on its financial services sector. GDP was growing at 7.2 percent in 2016, while inflation fell to 2 percent. Government debt – the ultimate target of most austerity policies – was also falling steadily, from 68.1 percent of GDP in 2015 to 54.0 percent in 2016.

Policy assessment

There was clearly significant scope for things in Iceland to get far worse, for far longer, rather than to improve considerably, in even the medium term. The scale of the crisis, relative to the economy, forced a more fundamental rethink than many others had to face. Iceland's strong collective instinct also influenced its response.

Iceland was perhaps fortunate that the UK and Netherlands decided to push too hard for recompense for their investors – and that the legal judgement was that those debts were the responsibility of the banks alone, relieving the government of a large amount of debt. Tackling the crisis by maintaining the functionality of society helped Iceland recover, and ensured that its productive capacity was supported, rather than damaged further. Another significant factor is that austerity measures were borne largely by sectors that could best afford them – and even then, only when the economy was in recovery and well out of recession.

Considering the policy package as a whole, Iceland's response to the 2008 crisis was almost exactly the opposite of most other countries – with outcomes that also contrast sharply with those realized elsewhere.

The US Response and the Great Recession: "Austerity-lite"

The "Great Recession" – officially dating from December 2007 to June 2009 – was the longest and most serious US recession since the Great Depression, with the slowest recovery on record. It was characterized by lower GDP growth, reduced tax receipts, higher social welfare costs, and rising government deficits and debt. However, the dire effects on the financial services sector – the root cause of the recession – not only added some very expensive bank bailouts to the equation, but also raised questions of how to help the economy recover, without disregarding the problems of longer-term deficit and debt reduction.

Dealing with these problems was further complicated by the length of the recession, which provided the scope for considerable political churn, and several changes of government – not to mention overall political control in both houses of Congress – resulting in a succession of alternative political views, and hence policy. Austerity – in this case referred to as "sequestration" – would be part of the mix, but would never achieve anything like the policy dominance of austerity in Europe.

Policy aims

As in many Western economies at the time, stabilizing the financial sector was a major priority. However, the scale of funds required to do this effectively would add considerably to government debt, while the recession caused by the financial crisis would increase the deficit – adding further to national debt.

But unlike much of Europe, the American focus was not entirely on austerity as a result of increased public deficits and debt; it was also on employment, GDP growth, and the health of the economy generally. There was also a far more open discussion about how and when reducing government debt should be prioritized, with the then Chairman of the Federal Reserve System, Ben Bernanke, favoring a longer, more gradual approach, and the Republicans in Congress taking a much more hawkish view.

Overall, policy – to a large extent reflecting matching shifts in political influence – moved back and forth between relatively mild stimulus and "austerity lite," thereby illustrating the political dimensions of austerity.

Policy development

The catalyst for the Great Recession was the bursting of the American subprime mortgage bubble, which undermined the securitized products in which subprime mortgages were packaged, seriously damaging the financial institutions that held them. Facing a financial and economic crisis of unprecedented scale, the focus was initially on stabilizing the financial sector and preventing economic collapse. With that in mind, economists and policymakers resurrected Keynesian ideas about the stabilizing role of fiscal deficits; and in February 2008, with the support of both Democrat and Republican lawmakers, Republican President George W. Bush signed the Economic Stimulus Act into law. This provided rebates for low- and middle-income taxpayers, incentives to encourage business investment, and an increase in the limits imposed on mortgages eligible for purchase by the Federal National Mortgage Association ("Fannie Mae") and the Federal Home Loan Mortgage Association ("Freddie Mac"), which had suffered heavy losses (although this only made their balance sheets worse).

The stimulus program helped to support consumption and investment; but its impact on the stability of the financial sector was limited by further seismic events. In March, the investment bank Bear Sterns was rescued from bankruptcy and sold to J.P. Morgan; and in September, Fannie Mae and Freddie Mac were taken over by the US federal government. However, there was worse to come: That same month, Lehman Brothers, the fourth largest investment bank in the US, was allowed to fail. This caused panic in international financial markets, as banks looked to their governments for support. Fearing a possible collapse of the American financial system, in October 2008, the Emergency Stabilization Act was passed, creating the Troubled Asset Relief Program (TARP), which purchased toxic assets and equity from financial institutions, and rescued banks deemed "too big to fail."

In terms of monetary policy, the Fed lowered the federal funds rate from 5.25 percent in September 2007 to a range of 0–0.25 percent by December 2008. With the rate at its effective lower limit, the Federal Open Market Committee (FOMC) used its forward guidance to support monetary stimulus, by making reference to keeping the rate at an exceptionally low level "for some time." The Fed introduced various programs to reduce the cost of private credit and facilitate credit flows; and in late November, to help lower longer-term public and private borrowing rates, it also initiated the first program of "quantitative easing" ("QE1"), by buying mortgage-backed securities, consumer loans, and Treasury bills, bonds, and notes.

At this point, the first in a series of political changes arrived, with Bush being replaced by the Democrat President Barack Obama, and his party gaining control over both chambers of Congress. In January 2009, the newly elected administration faced an economy in recession, a battered financial sector, and an annual rate of job loss of 3.5 percent – the largest since 1939. Confronting a collapsing economy, the Obama government, Fed officials, and many private economists called for continued emergency stimulus; but opposition to this was strong.

On January 29, more than 200 economists signed a full-page ad in the *New York Times* arguing *against* stimulus, sponsored by the Cato Institute. The letter stated:

> Notwithstanding reports that all economists are now Keynesians and that we all support a big increase in the burden of government, we the undersigned do not believe that more government spending is a way to improve economic performance ... To improve the economy, policymakers should focus on reforms that remove impediments to work, saving, investment and production. Lower tax rates and a reduction in the burden of government are the best ways of using fiscal policy to boost growth.[2]

But undeterred, in February – with the aim of offsetting state and local spending cuts (because most states are required to balance their operating budgets each year) – the Obama administration enacted the American Recovery and Reinvestment Act (ARRA), to save existing jobs, create new ones as quickly as possible, provide temporary relief for those most affected and invest in infrastructure, education, health, and renewable energy.

These policies proved effective, with the recession ending in June that same year; and by 2010, a weak recovery was under way, with GDP growing at an annual rate of 2.5 percent (compared with a contraction of 2.8 percent in 2009). The rate of increase in unemployment – which had more than doubled between 2007 and 2009 (from 4.6 percent to 9.3 percent) – slowed. But economic weakness persisted and unemployment remained at historically high levels.

Although successful in their stated aims, the stimulus measures had also continued to expand public deficits and debt, with the government deficit amounting to 10.9 percent of GDP in 2010 (up from 2.9 percent in 2007), and the national debt reaching 95.8 percent of GDP (up from 64.6 percent 2007). This – now that concerns about financial collapse and depression had receded – became the new focus for policymakers.

In his January 2010 State of the Union Address, Obama complained that he had inherited "a government deeply in debt." While acknowledging that emergency stimulus and bank bailouts had "helped save jobs and avert disaster," he then argued for austerity, using the (by now well out-of-date) comparison of a household budget with that of a government:

> [F]amilies cross the country are tightening their belts and making tough decisions. The federal government should do the same ... Like any cash-strapped family, we will work within a budget to invest in what we need and sacrifice what we don't ... If we don't take meaningful steps to rein in our debt, it could damage our markets, increase the cost of borrowing, and jeopardize our recovery – all of which would have an even worse effect on our job growth and family incomes.[3]

Obama also argued for healthcare reform to help reduce the deficit, and in March 2010, social security provision was strengthened by the Patient Protection and Affordable Care Act (ACA) – nicknamed "Obamacare." With the 2010 amendment to the Health Care and Education Reconciliation Act, this represented the most significant overhaul of US healthcare coverage since the Social Security Amendments of 1965 had created Medicare and Medicaid.

Obama signaled his commitment to long-term debt reduction by creating the National Commission on Fiscal Responsibility and Reform, to identify "policies to improve the fiscal situation in the medium-term and to achieve fiscal sustainability over the long-run."[4] The Commission released its report in December 2010. However, although supported by eleven out of the eighteen Commission members, with an equal number of Democrats and Republicans, it did not reach the threshold required to go to Congress for approval.

Attention also turned to financial reform, to prevent any repeat of the events that had produced the financial crisis. The resulting 2010 Dodd–Frank Wall Street Reform and Consumer Protection Act brought the most significant changes to US financial regulation since the Great Depression.

Meanwhile, monetary and fiscal policy continued to be accommodative. The Fed announced a second round of quantitative easing ("QE2"), and, in December, the 2010 Tax Relief, Unemployment Insurance Reauthorization and Job Creation Act (also known as the Tax Relief Act) was passed. The Tax Relief Act continued the Bush tax cuts for two years, provided a one-year reduction in the FICA payroll tax, and extended parts of ARRA as well as unemployment benefits.

The Democrats' complete control of government, however, did not last. In the 2010 midterm elections, they lost control of the House of Representatives altogether, but retained a slim majority in the Senate. This abruptly shifted Obama's stance on fiscal stimulus, since he blamed the election results on the business community's fear of government deficits, debt, and regulation. This was reinforced by the newly energized Republicans who, now in control of the House and with increased influence in the Senate, used their new-found power to press for deficit and debt reduction.

This culminated in the 2011 "debt ceiling" crisis when, in May, the Treasury's borrowing had reached the limit set by Congress in February 2010. Normally, when this happens, the debt ceiling is simply raised, without partisan debate or further terms and conditions. However, this time, House Republicans demanded spending cuts in return for raising it. The crisis continued until two days before the date the Treasury had estimated its borrowing authority would be exhausted.

On August 2, the Budget Control Act of 2011 was signed into law, creating the Congressional Joint Selection Committee on Deficit Reduction and introducing options for a balanced budget amendment, with automatic budget "sequestration," limiting the size of government budgets, if no agreement on budget cuts of $1.2 trillion had been reached by December 2012. It also resolved the debt ceiling crisis by raising the ceiling to $400 billion, with immediate effect.

In September, while acknowledging the need for *long-term* deficit and debt reduction, monetary authorities warned that too much *short-term* fiscal restraint could undermine the recovery. Bernanke argued that "[a]cting now to put in place a credible plan for reducing future deficits over the long-term, while being attentive to the implications of fiscal choices for the recovery in the near-term, can help serve both objectives."[5]

His warning proved well founded. While the policy had been branded "sequestration" rather than "austerity," this made little difference to either the measures involved or their outcomes; and by the end of 2011, GDP growth had weakened and unemployment remained persistently high. The deficit had been only slightly reduced, so public debt rose further, reaching nearly 100 percent of GDP.

During the 2012 presidential election, deficits and debt continued to be major campaign issues, with monetary policy remaining accommodative. In September, a third round of quantitative easing ("QE-infinity") was announced – a $40-billion-per-month open-ended bond-purchasing program of agency mortgage-backed securities, later increased to $85 billion per month. Meanwhile the FOMC announced that it would maintain the federal funds rate near zero "at least through mid-2015."

Obama's re-election set-up further showdowns over public spending, with the first obstacle being a "fiscal cliff." At 12:01 a.m. Eastern Standard Time (EST) on January 1, 2013, the US "technically" went over it, when no agreement on the budget cuts mandated by the 2011 Budget Control Act had been reached. But by midnight, a compromise measure, the American Taxpayer Relief Act of 2012 (ATRA), was passed by Congress and signed into law the following day. ATRA partially resolved the fiscal cliff by addressing the expiration of the Bush tax cuts, which had been only temporarily extended by the 2010 Tax Relief Act. This made the lower rate effectively permanent, but retained the higher rates and limited tax deductions and credits for those at upper-income levels. The Act also delayed activation of the 2011 Budget Control Act's sequestration provisions.

But the debt ceiling was not changed, setting up a repeat of the protracted row two years previously. On December

31, 2012, the ceiling set in 2011 was reached and the Republicans again opposed raising it. They eventually relented and allowed a debt ceiling increase until May 2013, with the crisis finally being brought to an end on October 17, 2013, with passage of the 2014 Continuing Appropriations Act.

On February 26, 2013, shortly before the ATRA deadline for sequestration budget cuts – Bernanke had again warned Congress against the "sharp, front-loaded spending cuts" coming into effect, if no deal was reached to prevent them; and he urged that these be replaced "with policies that reduce the federal deficit more gradually in the near-term but more substantially in the long-run":

> The size of deficits and debts matter, of course, but not all tax and spending programs are created equal with respect to their effects on the economy. To the extent possible, in their efforts to achieve sound public finances, fiscal policy makers should not lose sight of the need for federal tax and spending policies that increase incentives to work and save, encourage investments in workforce skills, advance private capital formation, promote research and development, and provide necessary and productive private infrastructure. Although economic growth alone cannot eliminate federal budget imbalances ... a more rapidly expanding economic pie will ease the difficult choices we face."[6]

However, on March 1, 2013, with no deal reached, Obama signed the sequester cuts into effect.

In a rare example of bipartisanship – and with the aim of avoiding another disruptive government shutdown – Republican House Budget Committee Chairman Paul Ryan, together with his Senate counterpart Democrat Patty Murray, negotiated a compromise agreement. And in December 2013, Congress approved the Bipartisan Budget Act, which rolled back sequestration cuts to education, medical research, infrastructure, and homeland security for fiscal years 2014 and 2015, in exchange for extending cuts to mandatory spending into 2022 and 2023, and making savings elsewhere.

This partially reversed the deficit reduction scheme, effectively putting an end to austerity, economically, if not politically. As a consequence, by the end of 2014, the economy was growing at 2.4 percent and unemployment had fallen to

6.2 percent. With improvement in the economy, the deficit also fell, although public debt continued to rise (to 105.07 percent of GDP), since the deficit had not been turned to surplus.

The following year, Obama announced an end to "mindless austerity" since it could have "serious consequences for our national security, at a time when our military is stretched on a whole range of issues."[7] Thus, by 2016, deficit and debt reduction had disappeared as political and campaign issues.

Policy assessment

Overall, the effects of stimulus and sequestration (austerity) were largely what would have been expected. Stimulus contributed to improvements in employment and economic growth during the recession; but it also, in the short term at least, added to the government's deficit and debt. By contrast, sequestration slowed GDP growth, with a damaging effect on employment; but (in the context of recovery), the deficit was indeed reduced. However, it is important to remember that for deficit reduction to translate into lower public debt, it needs to be replaced by a sustained surplus, which is extremely difficult – if not impossible – to achieve in the short term, particularly in the absence of exceptionally strong growth.

The most significant factor in the American response to the Great Recession, however, is, once again, timing. The initial response was emergency stimulus, which was successful in keeping the economy on its feet and supporting recovery. By the time sequestration appeared in the policy mix, the economy was growing again – albeit not especially strongly. Consequently, the brake austerity put on the economy was relatively gentle (if still unwelcome).

Conclusions

Iceland is unique amongst the countries in the front line of the 2008 financial crisis, as the Icelandic banks were wound up en masse, not least because their combined balance sheets were so much larger than the overall economy. In spite of the rhetoric in the UK and the US – about banks and financial systems being "too big to fail" – Iceland had little choice and was forced to find out what would happen if they did indeed fail. It therefore took a very different attitude to the moral hazard question, laying the blame – and the burden – squarely with the lenders, rather than forcing taxpayers – and society – to bear the cost.

The Icelandic economy is now no worse-off than that of Ireland, and probably for similar reasons. The emphasis was on growth, with only modest changes to public spending and taxation, the burden of which was borne by those most able to afford it. However, in the case of Ireland, investors emerged mostly unscathed, whereas in Iceland, they paid the price for excessive risk-taking.

In the US case, the American response was neither consistent nor well planned; and its evolution through numerous political changes meant that, sooner or later, some sort of austerity would be involved. As it happened, it was later, by which time a reasonable recovery was under way. As a result, the modest austerity that was actually implemented had little negative impact on the economy.

The cases of Iceland and the US both clearly demonstrate that concentrating on economic fundamentals is the most effective way to manage public deficits and debt. Both countries focused on the *objectives* of austerity (reduction of deficit and debt), but did so by prioritizing growth, rather than spending cuts and tax hikes; they also delayed austerity – deliberately or by chance – until the economy had strengthened enough to support it. This is a vital point, demonstrating that there is nothing the matter with austerity as a policy – or with its objectives of reducing public deficits and debt. The problem is with the timing, since, if austerity – rather than measures designed to restart growth – is applied during a recession, the result will always be counterproductive.

Aside from pure economics, the influence of culture and politics is also apparent. In America, the initial response was made with a Republican in the White House – the Republicans being the party that can usually be counted on to back spending cuts. Memories of the Wall Street Crash and the Great Depression which followed it likely played a part in the decision to stimulate the economy, rather than cutting spending.

In the case of Iceland, being far smaller makes reaching general policy decisions much easier; and the closely interrelated nature of Icelandic society encourages prioritization of societal outcomes. These factors, which may at first appear relatively insignificant by comparison to some of the more technical economic reasons for adopting a particular policy – like austerity – nonetheless exerted a powerful influence on the choice of policy direction and, hence, the outcomes achieved.

9
Austerity's Political Economic, Ideological, and Sociocultural Dimensions

Introduction

As an economic policy, austerity has a very limited track record of success; it also usually comes with significant side effects, particularly in terms of its impact on an economy and society when implemented during a recession – which it usually is. In spite of this, the idea has proven persistent, which is an interesting question in itself – and one we will grapple with in this chapter.

We therefore now return to the arguments used to justify austerity – in the light of our case studies – before considering the political economic, ideological, and sociocultural dimensions of austerity. Our ultimate objective is to gain an understanding of why – despite its repeated failure to deliver on its promises – austerity remains such a tenacious idea and policy.

The Arguments Used to Justify Austerity: In the Light of Economic History and Events

As we have seen, austerity is neither a well worked-out body of economic theory nor a sharply defined and coherent set of economic policies. Since the emergence of national debt some three hundred years ago, the debate about austerity has followed an evolving set of economic problems – mainly relating to public debt. Surprisingly, many of the arguments in support of austerity are still based on much earlier ideas, despite the significant changes in the way that public debt is accumulated and the uses to which it is put.

Having examined the main arguments and counterarguments – and then evaluated them in the context of the comparative case studies – it is time to revisit these ideas, with the aim of considering what they tell us about austerity, as both a political idea and an economic policy.

The 90 percent public debt-to-GDP "stagnation" threshold

One influential argument in support of austerity – based on the public debt-to-GDP ratio and Reinhart and Rogoff's historical research – claimed to identify a level of public debt (90 percent of GDP) at which economic growth contracts. Although the evidence for this "stagnation threshold" has since been completely discredited, with even the direction of causation being questioned, as we saw in the post-2008 case studies, it was widely used to justify austerity – and still is. According to this argument, any country with a debt-to-GDP ratio of 90 percent or more should implement austerity as a means of reducing public debt to a growth-supporting level.

However, although this ratio is useful for tracking trends in a government's financial balance, it should be interpreted with significant caution. Weimar Germany between the two world wars, as well as Iceland, Ireland, and Greece during the decade preceding the 2008 financial crisis, all experienced what looked like stellar growth, encouraging further capital inflows that provided the ability to service any public debts without difficulty. But the funds needed for debt servicing were abruptly cut off with the arrival of the 1929 stock market crash and the 2008 financial crisis, respectively. This caused sharply increasing public debt-to-GDP ratios, due to both recession (causing a fall in GDP and rising government deficits) and increased public debt.

Elsewhere though – notably in postwar Japan, Britain, and America – public debt-to-GDP ratios far beyond 90 percent have clearly not been a major problem. In the case of Japan, the vast majority of the government's debt is held by its own citizens, rather than by potentially hostile international investors. Also, unlike members of the Eurozone, these three countries have a sovereign currency, with a floating exchange rate; so regardless of the level of debt, there is no *actual* risk of default. This is partly because the debt is in the government's own currency, more of which can be created if required; and, if necessary, there is also the option of devaluation to make repayments more affordable.

It is therefore clear that there is no simple rule, based on the public debt-to-GDP ratio, for determining the sustainability – or otherwise – of a government's debt.

Likening a government to a private sector budget

One of the oldest and most persistent arguments for austerity is that a government's budget can be meaningfully compared to that of a private household or business – and that both require balancing. After all, when an individual, household, or business has too much debt, it makes sense to stop spending and "tighten the belt" – so why shouldn't governments do the same? Following the 2008 crisis, because of its intuitive appeal, this was one of the most powerful arguments used by politicians and the media to persuade the public that austerity was necessary.

The problem with this analogy is that it no longer makes the *economic* sense it once did – when governments accumulated debt to fund temporary wars, were not yet reliant on income tax and had no permanent commitment to welfare. As governments assumed responsibility for social security, and income tax became an important source of revenue, the dynamics of government deficits, debt, stimulus, and austerity began to behave in entirely new ways. Although spending cuts by households or businesses affect very few others, austerity will cause many to reduce spending at the same time – and as de Mandeville and Keynes argued, that leaves nothing to stimulate investment – so we cannot all cut our way to growth at the same time. Worse still, when a government – whose budget often represents a significant proportion of GDP – cuts spending, almost everyone is affected.

The case studies do, however, suggest that there is indeed a link between national debt and household or business debt – but in terms of its *affordability*, rather than its *level*. Just as an adequate and secure means of servicing a loan is (in theory, at least) part of the process for allocating private debt, it has similar implications for the sustainability of public debt.

As discussed above, the cases of postwar America, Britain, and, especially, Japan, demonstrate that public debt-to-GDP ratios far in excess of the fabled 90 percent can be entirely supportable, given the appropriate underlying economic structure to facilitate servicing the debt. Conversely, Ireland and Greece following the 2008 financial crisis – as well as Weimar Germany – all clearly illustrate the potentially devastating consequences of the abrupt loss of the means of servicing debt. The same thing contributed to the failure of many financial institutions during the 2008 crisis; and an individual trying to service debts following redundancy would confront a similar problem.

"Crowding-out"

"Crowding-out" is another argument for austerity, dating back to David Ricardo and the classical political economists of the eighteenth and nineteenth centuries. The idea is that government borrowing diverts resources from the private sector, "crowding-out" private investment. Worse still, by competing with private investors for a limited supply of funds, the theory also suggests that borrowing costs will rise, causing a further reduction in private investment. Governments should therefore reduce borrowing – in other words, opt for austerity.

However, this argument, too, has been largely overtaken by economic and financial developments. Since the 1970s, deregulated global finance and capital flows, along with high levels of saving in countries like China, have provided the credit to fund the debt of many nations – with more than enough left over to fuel regular asset bubbles. There is therefore no shortage of credit; but there will be a lack of demand for it when a bubble bursts.

Some have also suggested the possibility of "psychological" (rather than financial) "crowding-out." From this perspective, increased public debt undermines confidence in a government's ability to service its debts, increasing the perceived risk of default. In response, investors demand a higher return, triggering a vicious cycle of rising borrowing costs, deficits, and debt – with austerity prescribed as the solution to the problem. However, while "psychological crowding-out" might conceivably apply within the Eurozone, as discussed above, a country with control over its currency and a floating exchange rate is at no *real* risk of default; so austerity can safely be postponed until GDP growth is strong enough to withstand it.

Yet another variant of "crowding-out" is the idea that the anticipation of lower *future* taxes, made possible by reducing public debt, will raise private sector confidence. Austerity will therefore cause an increase in *current* private investment and consumption, more than it will offset the drop in government spending, which, in turn, will boost GDP growth, meaning that austerity could actually be "expansionary."

However, as well as the dynamics of national accounting and the fiscal multiplier, the case studies suggest that there are major difficulties with this idea. As we have seen, unless the economy is expanding and the fiscal multiplier is low (if not negative), austerity can be expected to *slow* (rather than increase) growth. Only in very specific (and extremely unusual) circumstances – when GDP growth is strong and other economic fundamentals are favorable – might "expansionary fiscal contraction" be, theoretically at least, possible.

As the cases also show, the direction of causation is usually the other way around – with sustainable growth permitting austerity to be effective in reducing public debt. This was the case in Ireland, before and after the 2008 crisis, as well as in Iceland and the United States after it. In each, the economy was growing, or at least on a sustainable recovery path, *before* austerity was implemented. This made it possible to turn budget deficits to surplus allowing, in turn, the reduction of public debt. It is therefore clear, that sustainable GDP growth makes it possible to reduce public debt through austerity, rather than austerity driving GDP growth and facilitating deficit and debt reduction. In this, the timing of austerity is critical.

Countercyclical vs Counterproductive Economic Policy

Another significant theme – also involving the public debt-to-GDP ratio – offers insight into the likely effectiveness of austerity in achieving its (stated, at least) objectives. A common stated objective of austerity is economic growth, seen to be achieved through public deficit and debt reduction and/or wage and price controls to promote business and export competitiveness. According to this logic, austerity will have a positive effect on GDP growth, if public deficit and debt reduction inspire investor confidence, resulting in increased productive investment, which, in turn, sets off a virtuous cycle of increasing employment, incomes, and domestic consumption, adding to GDP, and permitting further reductions in public debt.

Following the 2008 crisis, since the economic problem was quickly re-redefined as one of debt (rather than growth), austerity was focused on reducing that debt. But success proved elusive; and most countries have not only failed to achieve sustainable levels of economic growth, they also still have very high levels of public debt.

As we have seen, two or more successive quarters of negative GDP growth puts an economy officially into recession. In this context, assuming that there is already a national debt, it will almost certainly increase sharply, causing an abrupt worsening of the public debt-to-GDP ratio. If politicians, without a clear understanding of the economic dynamics involved, then use the ratio as a one-off indicator of the government's debt position, the result is likely to be a counterproductive (rather than well-considered) policy reaction.

As the cases consistently demonstrate, GDP growth is far more likely to contribute to a reduction in national debt than the other way around. We saw this in Weimar Germany, Britain, and America between the two world wars, as well as in Ireland (during the 1980s and following the

2008 crisis), postwar Japan, and Iceland and the United States after the 2008 crisis. By contrast, Greece and the UK, following the 2008 crisis, starkly demonstrate the consequences of attempting to reduce public debt in the absence of sustainable growth.

A recession, by definition, means that GDP growth has dropped, which, in turn, reduces government income at the same time as social costs are rising. This, in itself, is hardly good news; but if austerity is applied at this point in the economic cycle, it will magnify both effects – especially if the public sector represents a significant part of the economy. Nor is there much help to be expected from "expansionary austerity," as discussed above. Aside from there very rarely being a shortage of credit, one of the main features of a recession is a lack of confidence – and it is likely to be this, as much as anything, that will inhibit private investment during a downturn. As we saw in Chapter 3 on national accounting, under these circumstances, both deficits and accumulated debt will usually rise. Austerity therefore amounts to a *counterproductive* economic policy intervention.

However, since GDP growth (as opposed to debt reduction) has a larger – and rapid – effect on the public debt-to-GDP ratio, policies that will encourage GDP to rise as strongly and as soon as possible make considerable sense. Given the lack of business confidence that typically accompanies a recession, there is thus a role for the public sector to play as an investor – which can be expected, at some point, to contribute to an improvement in private sector confidence. After all, it is not just financial markets that are subject to Keynes's famous "animal spirits." It was Keynes, amongst others, who, during the interwar years, recognized that economic dynamics had changed. In the context of recession, they recommended stimulus (rather than austerity), with austerity being the policy for the boom, to provide resources to counter the next slump. In other words, they called for *countercyclical*, rather than counterproductive, economic policy.

The cases discussed above also bear this out – especially the opposing experiences of the United States and the United Kingdom post-2008. While the US opted for stimulus, maintaining it until growth was re-established – and only then, briefly, imposing a mild form of austerity – the UK embraced austerity, when only a stuttering recovery was in progress – choking it off. Predictably, US growth continued at acceptable, if not stellar, levels, while the UK endured a lengthy recession.

Clearly then, austerity will be effective only if growth is strong enough to turn the government deficit into surplus for long enough to allow debt reduction. Otherwise, austerity usually makes things worse – economically, socially, and politically – particularly if austerity causes public debt to remain high (or to rise further) and GDP growth to remain weak (or to fall), or if those being asked to pay either cannot do so, or perceive it as unfair.

Our examination of economic theory and history – as well as comparative case studies – however, strongly suggests that economic explanations, in themselves, are not enough to account for the persistence of austerity, both as an idea and a policy. The debate about austerity is therefore wider than the economics of it. So we now turn to some of the political economic, ideological, and sociocultural dimensions of austerity, in search of explanations for its tenacity.

The Political Economics of Austerity

Some have argued that the rise of austerity is rooted in the broader hollowing-out of Western democratic politics, where politicians take advantage of crises as opportunities to pursue objectives – such as using austerity to reduce the size and economic role of the state – which would not otherwise be politically possible. Mark Blyth describes this as a form of "political opportunism."[1]

In this context, austerity is often portrayed in ways that resonate with people who might find economics difficult to access, and are therefore likely to shun abstract economic concepts in favor of intuitively appealing ideas about the economy and a government's budget – such as likening them to a household or private business – which they understand and can identify with. They also tend to take their cue from authoritative opinion leaders whom they identify as having their interests at heart or who sound plausible. In this, the media has played a role in reproducing the idea that public deficits and debt are de facto "bad," regardless of the economic reality, thereby reinforcing the public's skepticism about government intervention.

Political ideology thus plays a part, often founded on objections to public debt on principle, fear of what the result of an expanded state role in the economy and society might be, and the view that free markets provide optimal economic efficiency, while government simply gets in the way.

Wolfgang Streeck sees austerity as a political problem of distribution – rather than an economic problem of national accounting – in "democratic capitalism," which embodies two competing principles of distribution, one (democratic politics) delivering social justice and the other (capitalist markets) delivering economic justice.[2] From this perspective, the accumulation of debt (both public and private) was the way by which capitalist democracies postponed the crisis of growth that had started in the 1970s.

As we saw in the case studies, during the 1990s, governments came under pressure from private creditors to reduce their debt by means of austerity. In this context, politicians – aware that austerity policies went against society's democratic claims for social justice – found a compromise in what Colin Crouch described as "privatized Keynesianism," the replacement of public debt with private debt.[3] For Streeck, this was a policy of "buying time"; and since the 2008 crisis, we have been continuing to buy time through quantitative easing. But we cannot buy time forever: as we have seen, continuing high levels of public debt since the 2008 crisis have put politicians under pressure to credibly commit to fiscal responsibility through potentially unpopular policies like austerity. Mark Blyth describes this as "*austerity as payback* – payback for a failed attempt to substitute monetary growth for real growth."[4]

Austerity's Ideological and Cultural Dimensions

Although austerity has rarely achieved its objectives – stated or otherwise – its ideology remains very powerful; and mounting evidence of the economic damage, social unrest, and political instability it has usually resulted in has so far failed to change this. Even though the IMF, one of its most influential proponents, has recently published reports acknowledging austerity's self-defeating character[5] – arguing that countries should relax or postpone it until their economies are better able to withstand it – austerity remains.

In his 2013 book, *Austerity: The History of a Dangerous Idea*, Mark Blyth points out that "facts never disconfirm a good ideology," highlighting the rhetorical power of austerity. From this perspective, austerity is intuitively and politically appealing as a response to the problem of excessive debt, both private and public. Again, the cases bear out the ideological strength of austerity. In Greece, for example, despite the obvious social, political, and economic damage austerity has caused, these programs have been lengthened and targets adjusted. But the underlying logic remains intact. In the UK, although austerity is now rarely mentioned in the media or political rhetoric, it remains firmly on the agenda. By contrast, the US publicly abandoned "mindless austerity" in 2015, seeing it as a potential threat to homeland security due to its economic, social, and political drawbacks.

Liam Stanley suggests that the narration of the 2008 crisis as a "debt crisis" made the idea of austerity both a logical and a common-sense solution to "living beyond our means."[6] From this perspective, the shared experience of the financialization of everyday life since the 1970s – and the tendency to make sense of government policies and anticipated outcomes through the lens of personal experiences – leads to a cultural predisposition toward seeing deficit-cutting as a sensible response to a moralized problem of government overspending. People's shared experiences of perceived overspending – and related feelings of guilt – thus help explain societal acceptance of austerity, despite its adverse effects. In this context, "living within one's means" makes common sense, even if it doesn't necessarily make economic sense.

Sociocultural norms also have an influence on attitudes about austerity. The case studies demonstrate that austerity tends to be more common and extensive in countries with a culture based on the individual (such as the US, the UK, and parts of Latin America) than in those with a more collectivist culture (like Iceland and Japan). In individualistic cultures, austerity remains electorally powerful, despite evidence that it worsens the economy and exacerbates inequality. This is partly explained by the reconceptualization of poverty and unemployment as the fault of the victims and/or government interference with market forces, as opposed to a predictable outcome of the market economy, in need of state intervention, since the 1970s and 1980s. In this context, austerity meets the political goal of welfare reform aimed at reducing the size and economic role of the state by blaming the government – and casting poverty and unemployment as inferior moral, as opposed to material, conditions.

The Class Analytics of Austerity

Who benefits and who does not is another recurring theme in the debate about austerity. The case studies again clearly show that if cuts in social security for the most vulnerable in society are imposed on an economy in recession, the result will be rising unemployment, poverty, inequality, and socioeconomic hardship. This idea has recently been reinforced by reports from influential international organizations – including the IMF and Oxfam – drawing attention to the high, and rising, inequality caused by austerity, as well as its damaging effects on both social cohesion and economic growth.

IMF research identifies income *equality* as by far the most significant factor supporting sustainable economic growth; and it shows that, while the benefits from lower inequality are shared by most income groups, extreme inequality has historically resulted in crises, with the current rise being "strikingly similar" to that of the turbulent interwar years. "In both cases, there was a boom in the financial sector, poor people borrowed a lot, and a huge financial crisis ensued."[7] The IMF report concludes that "the recent global economic crisis ... may have resulted, in part at least, from the increase in inequality."[8]

Another report, this time by Oxfam, notes that since the 1980s, wealth and inequality have both risen to "levels never before seen ... [and] are getting worse."[9] It argues that extreme wealth and inequality are "economically inefficient," "politically corrosive," and "socially divisive." Because the wealthy do not spend as high a proportion of their income as those less well-off, excessive inequality depresses demand, slowing economic development and growth. Inequality can also help secure excessive political influence for the wealthy, through lobbying or corruption. It is also socially divisive, since some have private access to services that the majority depend upon the state to provide; and they then lobby for withdrawal of support for those public services.

On the surface, the persistence of austerity goes against the conventional wisdom of political economy, which suggests that voters will punish governments for not delivering growth, for cutting social spending, and for raising taxes. So, motivated by a desire to avoid blame, politicians can be expected to look for ways of legitimating these policies, when they can't be economically justified, and for building support for them.

One such political strategy is "divide and conquer," targeting cuts on weaker and less politically important groups to appease others. Another is to target already stigmatized social groups in an effort to build cross-cutting constituencies of beneficiaries with a common cause. An example of this could be to focus on the uses and abuses of taxpayers' money. We saw this in the case of the US under Reagan and following the 2008 crisis and in the UK post-2008. In both cases, austerity was portrayed as making life fairer for hard-working taxpayers – who pay their own way – as opposed to the "morally undeserving" rich (financial actors and institutions) or poor (welfare claimants) – who take more than their fair share from the public purse.[10]

But who benefits from austerity policies – and how might this explain why the world keeps returning to them? The case studies show that, as a consequence of austerity, those at the upper levels of the distribution of income and wealth have seen a significant increase in their asset wealth. Austerity has also benefited corporate actors – not least finance capital (financial speculators, banks, and their shareholders) – and creditors, focused on debt repayment. We saw this in the interwar cases and again following the 2008 crisis, when these groups had a dominant influence on policy.

But since austerity is intended to reduce public spending and debt, the logic of using public funds to rescue financial institutions deemed "too big to fail" cannot go unquestioned. An important contributor to the 2008 financial crisis was irresponsible lending to individuals, other financial institutions, and sovereign nations. From a moral hazard perspective, there is clearly a case for suggesting that the consequences of such behavior should fall on the private institutions involved (rather than the public sector and taxpayers), thus ruling out austerity. However, we saw this only in the case of Iceland's response to the 2008 crisis.

The clear losers from austerity are workers – especially those in the public sector – and groups within society that are most reliant on public services. Many of the case studies showed that, as a result of austerity, the vast majority of workers suffered income stagnation, if not reduction, leading to falling living standards and economic insecurity, with the potential to fuel social and political instability. Weimar Germany is perhaps the most extreme example of this, with deep and sustained austerity not only failing to resolve the country's economic problems, but also ratcheting up social tensions – and helping pave the way for the election of Hitler's Nazi party. But violence can cut both ways with austerity. In Pinochet's Chile – an equally extreme example, but this time motivated by concern over socialist revolution – any opposition was suppressed by armed force.

More recently, the UK Labour Party has been moved decisively to the left, chiefly by those experiencing the brunt of austerity measures. Greece, too, has seen widespread social and political unrest, as a result of the deep cuts imposed by the Troika; and Europe as a whole has experienced wide-ranging social and political movements, often labeled "populism." However, in Ireland and Iceland, where austerity was applied only after a sustainable recovery was under way – with the burden being borne by those who could best afford it – there was little, if any, public or political reaction.

The message, then, seems clear: Social security does *actually* benefit an economy as a whole, as it helps to maintain social, industrial, political, and economic stability – along with the health and well-being of the less well-off. Without such stability, the case studies discussed in Chapters 5–8 demonstrate how some very challenging economic, social, and political conditions can emerge – and surprisingly quickly.

Conclusions

The economic rationale for austerity cannot explain its strength as an idea and a policy. Perhaps this is because austerity offers an intuitively appealing solution to high levels of debt, largely ignores the complexity of the problem, and provides an apparently logical solution: if you have too much debt, stop spending so much. But this fails to engage with the radically altered dynamics of public finances following the introduction of both social security and income tax.

Austerity also resonates with ethical and moral attitudes toward debt – often being regarded as the "pain" necessary to atone for the excesses of "immoral" over-consumption following a bubble's collapse. A more constructive way of thinking about austerity might be that "prevention is better than cure." When an economy is overheating or an asset bubble is inflating, it is better to deflate it *then*, rather than wait until it bursts and try to deal with the (more costly) consequences. But, as we have seen, the use of austerity to cool an overheating economy or deflate an asset bubble often meets with both social and political resistance.

Austerity also makes more sense, if the point of view of particular segments of the economy – like finance – are taken in isolation, or if the economy is considered separately from society. This underlines the fact that one of the reasons for the persistence of austerity is the economic and political influence of its chief beneficiaries. For the small segment at the upper end of the distribution of income and wealth – which holds financial investments and assets, but has little reliance on debt or public services – a small state focused on low inflation might well make sense. However, for most, this brings major problems, particularly for those in low-paid, precarious employment, with growing debt burdens and difficulty maintaining living standards. Worse still, compared with the wealthy, this group will need more support in terms of welfare, pay little (if any) tax, and have limited ability to consume – all of which will, in turn, undermine economic growth still further.

Since the 2008 crisis, austerity has been critiqued for not only *not* achieving its stated economic aims and worsening the problems it is supposed to solve, but also for entrenching gender inequalities, disproportionately affecting disadvantaged groups, damaging public health, and undermining democratic capitalism. As the post-2008 case studies – as well as those of earlier periods – demonstrate, when austerity has been implemented during a recession or fragile recovery, it has increased inequalities in both wealth and power more than strengthened state finances through fiscal consolidation. Regardless of whether austerity was forced (as in the Eurozone) or voluntary (as in the US and the UK), in the absence of social protection for the most vulnerable in society, it has resulted in growing inequalities of wealth and power.

And yet, austerity persists as both a powerful ideology and policy, which begs the (perhaps unanswerable) question of the extent to which its damaging effects on society are worth it or not.

10
Conclusions

In the first part of this book, we considered the implications – in terms of both theory and policy – of national debt in its modern form, along with its counterpart, austerity. A number of ideas in support of austerity were discussed; but, as the comparative case studies show, without reference to economic history – and how those ideas have played out in reality – it is extremely difficult to assess them accurately.

The cases chosen all postdate World War I. This is because the nature of the state and uses to which public debt has been put, the supply of credit, the structure of society, as well as the nature and dynamics of the economy itself had all changed beyond recognition since the time of Adam Smith and his contemporaries, who were among the first to theorize austerity. When they were writing, public debt was mainly used to fund temporary military activities.

But with the emergence of large numbers of increasingly organized urban poor – and the possibility of socialist revolution – funding the welfare state increasingly became a means of avoiding potentially uncontrollable social, industrial, and political instability. Unlike war, which involved a limited financial obligation by the state, this meant a permanent commitment to the cost of social security; and, as we saw in the comparative case studies, reducing this commitment through austerity has often proved – even to the present day – a risky move.

We therefore conclude by returning to the point made in Chapter 1 – that the important question is *not* whether austerity is a "good" or a "bad" policy in terms of its effect on economic growth, or social and political stability. A better question is: "Under what circumstances might austerity be appropriate (and effective) – and when is it more likely to be counterproductive?"

It is clear from our examination of the many facets of austerity that economics is not a precise science and has few absolute rules. In most cases, the exact outcome of economic policy – including austerity – is difficult, if not impossible, to predict. This was well demonstrated by the IMF, whose estimate of the fiscal multiplier in 2010 turned out to be significantly wide of the mark. While this might well have been apparent after the event, it was far from obvious while trying to calculate the strength and likely economic impact of its austerity proposals.

This is why ideas created in think-tanks and universities – or indeed anywhere else – should be assessed against the record of economic history. But even then, there is not always a clearcut, "right" answer. Considering our examples of austerity in action, it is clearly possible to arrive at a practical assessment of austerity – as well as how and when it should be implemented. Even so, it will still be difficult to be precise about the extent of austerity's effects, despite the fact that their direction may be far more predictable. The justification for any economic policy will also often be clouded by political considerations, which is more than amply illustrated by economic history. Thus, the answer to the question of whether or not austerity is a useful policy will inevitably be: "It depends."

From a purely economic point of view, the dynamics of the economic cycle, and their effect on government finance through the sectoral balances model, suggest that, in a recession, austerity will *not* have the desired effects of reducing public deficits and debt; nor will it contribute to economic growth. That would require turning any deficit into a sustained surplus, which is difficult when both the recession and the automatic stabilizers are already working against you. However, in the growth phase of the cycle – the boom – there is greater scope for reducing debt, as more money is coming into the public purse while fewer demands are being made upon it.

The right time to apply austerity – which will generate funds for the next stimulus – is therefore a well-established expansion. But, as we have seen, this will, more likely than not, tend to be met with social and political resistance. Thus, while applying austerity during a recession is likely to have very predictable – and destabilizing – economic and social results, during a sustainable expansion it will be not only much more effective in achieving its key economic aims, but any social or political impact will be far less apparent to those who might, under different circumstances, protest.

In the end, as we have seen, the best means of addressing government deficits and debt is through sustainable growth, which puts a premium on the political choices and policies that support this. The interwar cases show that, after World War I, creditors – whose main objective was getting their money back – wrote policy; the result was significant damage to growth, economic and social chaos, and ultimately another world war. After that war, the allies instead wrote off enormous amounts of debt, particularly that of Germany. This was a *political* choice that made postwar growth possible.

Following the 2008 crisis – especially in Europe – the creditors are once again driving policy. However, much of the current debt and growth problem, as it was between the wars, is the result of financial crisis and recession, rather than structural factors. It can therefore be reversed – but only if there is the political will to do so.

To answer the question raised above – "When is austerity appropriate, and when is it more likely to be counterproductive?" – there is little doubt that austerity is far more likely to achieve its objectives of public deficit and debt reduction – and ultimately economic growth – during a boom or established recovery, when GDP growth is strong enough to support it and when protections are in place to support the most vulnerable in society. And austerity is more likely to be counterproductive during a recession or a recovery that is not strong enough to withstand it.

However, perhaps the most significant lesson to take away from our examination of austerity – in theory, policy, and action – is the same as for any other economic policy: Before committing to an idea – and the policies informed by it – take a long, hard look at economic history, and check how well the theory fits with the reality.

Notes

Chapter 1   Introduction

1   Keynes 1937.

Chapter 2   Shifting Responses to the Evolution of National Debt and the Economic Role of the State

1   Smith 2007 [1776], Book V, Chapter III; Hume 1742.
2   Smith 2007 [1776], p. 350.
3   Ricardo 1951–73, IV, p. 197.
4   McCullock 1871, p. 148.
5   Malthus 1836, p. 400.
6   Malthus 1836, p. 411.
7   Marx 1976, p. 919.
8   Marx 1976, p. 921.
9   Laidler 1999, p. 211.
10   Douglas and Director 1931, pp. 210–11.
11   Arndt 1972 [1944], p. 34.
12   Lerner 1943, p. 39.
13   Blyth 2013a, p. 738.
14   Blanchard et al. 2010, p. 7.
15   Greenspan 1999.
16   Reinhart and Rogoff 2010.
17   Osborne 2010.
18   Ryan 2013, p. 78.
19   Rehn 2013, p. 4.

20 Reinhart and Rogoff 2013.
21 Williamson 1990, p. 19.
22 Pender 2001, p. 399.
23 Ostry et al. 2016, p. 40.
24 Ostry et al. 2016, p. 41.

Chapter 3 National Accounting and the Economics of Austerity

1 Sargent 2013, p. 229.
2 Godley and Lavoie 2012 present a more complex elaboration of the underlying model.
3 IMF 2012, pp. 43–5.

Chapter 4 Selling Austerity: Economics, Politics, and Society

1 Cochrane 2009.
2 Fama 2009.
3 Quoted in Montopoli 2010.

Chapter 5 Austerity and Welfare: an Unstable Mixture

1 Quoted in Middlemas and Barnes 1969, p. 127.
2 Hawtrey 1925, p. 48.
3 Gregory et al. 1932.
4 Roosevelt 1936.

Chapter 6 Austerity (and Stimulus) in Postwar Chile, America, Ireland, and Japan

1 Quoted in Lewis 1975.
2 Arellano 1988, p. 19.
3 Friedman 1982, p. 59.
4 Petras et al. 1994, p. 27.
5 Foxley 1983, p. 103.
6 Petras et al. 1994, p. 33.
7 Ffrench-Davis 1988.
8 Petras et al. 1994, p. 34.

9 Diaz 1991, pp. 58–9; PET 1990, p. 192.
10 Reagan 1981.
11 Atkinson et al. 2017.
12 Quoted in Benenson 1984.
13 Unless otherwise indicated, from this point on, the case study data source for fiscal deficits is CountryEconomy.com 2018a and for public debt-to-GDP ratios is CountryEconomy.com 2018b.
14 Quoted in Lee 1993, p. 501.
15 Unless otherwise indicated, from this point on, the case study data source for unemployment, GDP, inflation, the balance of trade, and FDI is World Bank 2018.
16 Quoted in Takegawa 2013, p. 266.

Chapter 7 Some Have Austerity Thrust Upon Them, Others Embrace It

1 IMF 2018.
2 Hay 2013.
3 Skidelsky 2016, p. 36.
4 20 Economists 2010.
5 Cameron 2011.
6 Chick et al. 2016.
7 Balls 2014.

Chapter 8 Post-2008 Variations on Austerity

1 OECD 2018.
2 Cato Institute 2009.
3 Obama 2010a.
4 Obama 2010b.
5 Bernanke 2011.
6 Bernanke 2013.
7 Obama 2015.

Chapter 9 Austerity's Political Economic, Ideological, and Sociocultural Dimensions

1 Blyth 2013a, p. 738.
2 See, for example, Streeck 2014.

3   See, for example, Crouch 2009.
4   Blyth 2013a, p. 738.
5   IMF 2012; Ostry et al. 2016.
6   See Stanley 2014.
7   Berg and Ostry 2011, p. 15.
8   Berg and Ostry 2011, p. 13.
9   Oxfam 2013, p. 1.
10 See, for example, Stanley 2016.

References

20 Economists (2010) "UK Economy Cries Out for Credible Rescue Plan; LETTERS." *Sunday Times*, February 14, p. 28.

Arellano, José (1988) *Politicas Sociales y Desarrollo: Chile, 1924–1984*. Santiago: CIEPLAN.

Arndt, H.W. (1972 [1944]) *The Economic Lessons of the Nineteen-Thirties*. London: Frank Cass.

Atkinson, Tony, Joe Hassell, Salvatore Morelli, and Max Roser (2017) *Chartbook of Economic Inequality*. Oxford: Institute for New Economic Thinking. https://chartbookofeconomicinequality.com/wp-content/uploads/Chartbook_Of_Economic_Inequality_complete.pdf.

Balls, Ed (2014) "Can Labour Change Britain?" Speech to the Fabian Party Conference, January 25.

Benenson, R. (1984) "Social Welfare under Reagan." Editorial Research Reports 1984 (vol. I). Washington, DC: CQ Press. http://library.cqpress.com/cqresearcher/cqresrre1984030900.

Berg, Andrew, and Jonathan Ostry (2011) "Equality and Efficiency: Is There a Trade-off Between the Two or Do They Go Hand-in-Hand?" *Finance and Development*, September, pp. 12–15.

Bernanke, Ben (2011) "US Economic Outlook." Speech at the Economic Club of Minnesota Luncheon, Minneapolis, September 8.

Bernanke, Ben (2013) *Testimony: Semi-annual Monetary Policy Report to the Congress, Before the Committee on Banking, Housing and Urban Affairs*. Washington, DC: US Senate, February 26.

Blanchard, Olivier, G. Dell Ariccia, and P. Mauro (2010) "Rethinking Macroeconomic Policy." *IMF Staff Position Note SPN 10/03*, February 12.

Blyth, Mark (2013a) "Austerity as Ideology: A Reply to my Critics." *Comparative European Politics* 11, pp. 737–751.

Blyth, Mark (2013b) *Austerity: The History of a Dangerous Idea.* Oxford: Oxford University Press.

Cameron, David (2011) "David Cameron's Conservative Party Speech in Full." *Guardian*, October 5.

Cato Institute (2009) Advertisement. *New York Times*, January 9.

Chick, Victoria, and Ann Pettifor, with Geoff Tily (2016) *The Economic Consequences of Mr Osborne.* London: Policy Research in Macroeconomics.

Cochrane, John (2009) "Fiscal Stimulus, Fiscal Inflation or Fiscal Fallacies?" https://faculty.chicagobooth.edu/john.cochrane/research/papers/fiscal2.htm.

CountryEconomy.com (2018a) *[Country] Government Budget Deficit.* https://countryeconomy.com/deficit/[country].

CountryEconomy.com (2018b) *[Country] National Debt.* https://countryeconomy.com/national-debt/[country].

Crouch, C. (2009) "Privatized Keynesianism: An Unacknowledged Policy Regime." *British Journal of Politics and International Relations* 11(3), pp. 382–399.

Diaz, Alvaro (1991) *El Capitalismo Chileno en Los 90: Creimiento Economico y Disigualdad Social.* Santiago: Ediciones PAS.

Douglas, P.H., and A. Director (1931) *The Problem of Unemployment.* New York: Macmillan.

Fama, Eugene (2009) "Bailouts and Stimulus Plans." *Fama/French Forum*, January 13.

Ffrench-Davis, Ricardo (1988) *The Impact of Global Recession and National Policies on Living Standards: Chile, 1973–87.* Santiago: CIEPLAN.

Foxley, Alejandro (1983). *Latin American Experiments in Neoconservative Economics.* Oakland: University of California Press.

Friedman, Milton (1982) "Free Markets and the Generals." *Newsweek*, January 25, p. 59.

Godley, Wynne, and Marc Lavoie (2012) *Monetary Economics: An Integrated Approach to Credit, Money, Income, Production and Wealth*, 2nd edn. New York: Palgrave Macmillan.

Greenspan, Alan (1999) *Testimony of the Chairman of the Board of Governors of the US Federal Reserve System, Mr Alan Greenspan, before the Joint Economic Committee of the US Congress, June 17, 1999.* http://www.bis.org/review/r990707a.pdf.

Gregory, T.E., F.A. von Hayek, A. Plant, and L. Robbins (1932) "Spending and Saving: Public Works from Rates, to the Editor of the Times." *The Times*, October 19, p. 10, Issue 46268, Col. A.

Hawtrey, R.G. (1925) "Public Expenditure and the Demand for Labour." *Economica* 13, March, pp. 38–48.

Hay, Colin (2013) "Treating the Symptom Not the Condition: Crisis Definition, Deficit Reduction and the Search for a New British

Growth Model." *British Journal of Politics and International Relations* 15(1), pp. 23–37.

Hume, D. (1742) "Of Public Credit." *Essays, Moral, Political and Literary*. Indianapolis, IN: The Liberty Fund.

IMF (2012) *World Economic Outlook: Coping with High Debt and Sluggish Growth*. Washington, DC: International Monetary Fund.

IMF (2018) *Greece: Staff Concluding Statement of the 2018 Article IV Mission*. Washington, DC: International Monetary Fund.

Keynes, John Maynard (1937) "How to Avoid a Slump: 'Dear' Money, II. The Right Time for Austerity." *The Times*, January 13, p. 13, Issue 47581, Col. G.

Laidler D. (1999) *Fabricating the Keynesian Revolution: Studies of the Inter-War Literature on Money, the Cycle and Unemployment*. Cambridge: Cambridge University Press.

Lee, Joseph (1993) *Ireland Politics and Society 1912–1985*. Cambridge: Cambridge University Press.

Lerner, A. (1943) "Functional Finance and the Federal Debt." *Social Research* 10(1/4), pp. 38–51.

Lewis, Anthony (1975) "The Kissinger Doctrine." *New York Times*, February 27.

Malthus, Thomas (1836) *Principles of Political Economy*. London: William Pickering.

Marx, Karl (1976) *Capital: A Critique of Political Economy, Volume 1*. London: Pelican Books.

McCullock, J.R. (ed.) (1871) *The Works of David Ricardo*. London: John Murray.

Middlemas, Keith, and John Barnes (1969) *Baldwin: A Biography*. London: Macmillan.

Montopoli, Brian (2010) "Obama Proposes Freezing Federal Employee Pay." *CBS News*. November 29.

Obama, Barack (2010a) "The 2010 State of the Union Address." January 27.

Obama, Barack (2010b) *Executive Order 13531 – National Commission on Fiscal Responsibility and Reform*, February 18.

Obama, Barack (2015) *Remarks by the President on the Fiscal 2016 Budget*, February 2. Washington, DC: Department of Homeland Security.

OECD (2018) *OECD Income Distribution Database (IDD): Gini, Poverty, Income, Methods and Concepts*. Paris: Organisation for Economic Co-operation and Development.

Osborne, G. (2010) "A New Economic Model." Mais Lecture, February 24. https://conservative-speeches.sayit.mysociety.org/speech/601526.

Ostry, Jonathan, Prakash Loungani, and Davide Furceri (2016) "Neoliberalism: Oversold?" *Finance and Development*, June, pp. 38–41.

Oxfam (2013) "The Cost of Inequality: How Wealth and Income Extremes Hurt Us All." *Oxfam Media Briefing*, 18 January. Ref: 02/2013.

Pender, John (2001) "From 'Structural Adjustment' to 'Comprehensive Development Framework': Conditionality Transformed?" *Third World Quarterly* 22(3), pp. 397–411.

PET (1990) *Informe Annual*. Santiago: Programa de Economia del Trajabo.

Petras, James, Fernando Ignacio Leiva, and Henry Veltmeyer (1994) *Democracy and Poverty in Chile: The Limits to Electoral Politics*. Boulder, CO: Westview Press.

Reagan, Ronald (1981) "Inaugural Address." *The American Presidency Project*. https://www.presidency.ucsb.edu/node/246336.

Rehn, Olli (2013) "Deeper Integration in the Eurozone and Britain's Place in Europe." *Speech*, February 28. London: Policy Network Conference.

Reinhart, Carmen, and Kenneth Rogoff (2010) "Growth in a Time of Debt." *American Economic Review: Papers and Proceedings* 100, pp. 573–578.

Reinhart, Carmen, and Kenneth Rogoff (2013) "Debt, Growth and the Austerity Debate." *New York Times*, April 25.

Ricardo, David (1951–73) *Works and Correspondence of David Ricardo*, 11 vols., ed. Pierro Sraffa and Maurice Dobb. Cambridge: Cambridge University Press.

Roosevelt, F.D. (1936) "Address at Forbes Field, Pittsburgh, PA." *The American Presidency Project*. https://www.presidency.ucsb.edu/node/209177.

Ryan, Paul (2013) "Path to Prosperity: A Blueprint for American Renewal." *Fiscal Year 2013 Budget Resolution*. Washington, DC: House Budget Committee.

Sargent, Thomas (2013) *Rational Expectations and Inflation*, 3rd edn. Princeton, NJ: Princeton University Press.

Skidelsky, Robert (2016) "The Optimism Error." *The New Statesman* 145(5297), pp. 36–39.

Smith, Adam (2007 [1776]) *An Inquiry into the Nature and Causes of the Wealth of Nations*. New York: MetaLibri Digital Edition.

Stanley, Liam (2016) "Legitimacy Gaps, Taxpayers, Conflict and the Politics of Austerity in the UK." *British Journal of Politics and International Relations* 18(2), pp. 389–406.

Stanley, Liam (2014) "'We're Reaping What We Sowed': Everyday Crisis Narratives and Acquiescence to the Age of Austerity." *New Political Economy* 19(6), pp. 895–917.

Streeck, W. (2014) *Buying Time: The Delayed Crisis of Democratic Capitalism*. London: Verso.

Takegawa, Shogo (2013) "Change of Attitudes Towards Social Policy in Japan in the First Decade of the Twentieth Century: Neoliberalism or Welfare State?" *Development and Society* 42(4), pp. 263–286.

Williamson, John (1990) "What Washington Means by Policy Reform." In J. Williamson (ed.), *Latin American Adjustment: How Much has Happened?* Washington, DC: Institute for International Economics.

World Bank (2018) *World Development Indicators Databank.* http://databank.worldbank.org/data/reports.aspx?source=world-development-indicators#.

Index